God Wants You To Be Well

140655

104216

God Wants You To Be Well

Laurence H. Blackburn

Morehouse-Barlow Co.
Wilton, Connecticut

Paperback edition, second printing, 1976

Copyright © 1970 Morehouse-Barlow Co.
78 Danbury Road, Wilton, Connecticut 06897

Library of Congress Catalog Card No. 79-120337
Standard Book Number 8192-1079-X
Printed in the United States of America

Acknowledgements

The author wishes to thank the following proprietors for their generous permission to quote copyrighted material belonging to them:

The American Bible Society and William Collins & Sons Co., Ltd., for citations from *"Good News for Modern Man," The New Testament in Today's English Version,* Copyright 1966 by the American Bible Society.

The Old Testament Scripture quotations in this book are from the *Revised Standard Version of the Bible,* Copyright 1946 and 1952 by the Division of Christian Education of the National Council of Churches of Christ in the U.S.A., and used by permission.

The McGraw-Hill Book Company for excerpts from *The Miracle of Lourdes* by Ruth Cranston. Copyright 1955 by Ruth Cranston. Used with permission of the McGraw-Hill Book Company.

David McKay Company, Inc., for a definition from Horace B. English and Ava C. English, *A Comprehensive Dictionary of Psychological and Psychoanalytical Terms,* copyright 1958.

Faith at Work for quotations from an article by Frank B. Sladen that appeared in the issue for July/August 1958.

Abingdon Press for comments by George A. Buttrick and Vincent Taylor in Volume 7 of *The Interpreter's Bible,* copyright 1951 by Pierce and Smith.

Routledge & Kegan Paul Ltd. and Harcourt, Brace & World, Inc., for a quotation from Carl G. Jung's *Modern Man in Search of a Soul,* reprinted by permission of the publishers.

Lutterworth Press and John Knox Press for quotations from Bernard Martin's *The Healing Ministry in the Church,* copyright 1960 by Lutterworth Press.

The Epworth Press for quotations from W. L. Northridge's *Disorders of the Emotional and Spiritual Life,* copyright 1960 by The Epworth Press.

Forward Movement Publications for Alexis Carrel's *Prayer Is Power.*

W. B. Saunders Company for quotations from *Modern Clinical Psychiatry* (Fifth Edition), by Arthur P. Noyes and Laurence C. Kolb, copyright 1934, 1939, 1948, 1953, 1958 by W. B. Saunders Company.

Oxford University Press for quotations from Alan Richardson, *The Gospel and Modern Thought,* copyright 1950 by Oxford University Press.

SCM Press Ltd. for quotations from Alan Richardson, *The Miracle-Stories of the Gospels.*

Prentice-Hall, Inc., for material from John A. Schindler, *How to Live 365 Days a Year,* copyright 1954 by Prentice-Hall, Inc.

The publisher for material reprinted from *Medicine for Moderns* by Frank G. Slaughter, M.D., by permission of Julian Messner, a Division of Simon & Schuster, Inc. Copyright 1947 by Frank G. Slaughter.

Abingdon Press for quotations from Leslie D. Weatherhead's *Psychology, Religion and Healing* (Revised Edition), copyright 1951 by Pierce and Smith.

To my son
Laurence H. Blackburn, Jr., A.B., M.D., M.P.H.
Diplomate of the American Board of Preventive Medicine in
Aerospace Medicine.
Captain, Flight Surgeon, U.S. Navy

He makes his ministrations as a doctor
a ministry of healing of the whole man.

CONTENTS

INTRODUCTION

"How did you become interested in spiritual healing?"

Both publicly and privately this question has been put to me over and over again, and each time I have parried it, but quite unsuccessfully. I know the expected answer is that of some dramatic experience of healing for myself or someone close to me. Fortunately or unfortunately, there was no such event, so the story is exceedingly prosaic and most uninteresting, I am sure. But the question is important to many people. I will give you an honest answer, even though I know you will be disappointed, too!

While rector of St. Anne's Episcopal Church in Lowell, Massachusetts, I read several articles in religious magazines about spiritual healing and found them interesting to the point of resolving to follow up the subject "some day." However, this was continually postponed because I was without a curate during most of those war years in a large parish and, like so many ministers in downtown churches, I became involved in various civic affairs. One day the women in the parish (which proves how extensively spiritual healing is a laymen's movement!) invited the Rev. Robert M. Shaw, associate rector of Emmanuel Church in Boston, to give an address on the healing ministry he was conducting there. He gave a most inspiring and convincing presentation; the women were deeply impressed, and I firmly resolved to study the subject "at my earliest convenience." Parish "busyness" kept on apace, and eighteen months later I resigned my rectorship there to accept a call to another parish.

No information about the new parish warned me of what I was to learn when I walked into the office of Emmanuel Church in Cleveland, Ohio, on the Saturday before I was to begin my ministry there. Looking over the bulletin for Sunday I suddenly came upon this announcement:

Tuesday, 11:00 A.M. Holy Communion followed by a service of spiritual healing with the laying-on of hands.

I remember that I fairly shouted, "Why didn't someone tell me about this? I don't know anything about spiritual healing!" The secretary suggested that I ask the Rev. Andrew S. Gill, D.D., my predecessor, and retired, who lived in the city and who had started the healing ministry in the parish, to take the service on the next Tuesday and let me observe. This idea worked out happily, but the following Tuesday I was on my own. That, very simply, was my introduction to spiritual healing.

The need was apparent. The task was mine to do. I accepted the challenge. I read everything I could find on the subject. A week spent at the School of Pastoral Care conducted by Mrs. Agnes Sanford and her husband, the Rev. Edgar L. Sanford (since deceased), at Whitinsville,

Massachusetts, proved most helpful. The Conferences of the Order of St. Luke in St. Stephen's Church, Philadelphia, were inspiring. The Tuesday services increased in attendance, with one-third of the people coming from the parish, one-third coming from other Episcopal churches, and one-third coming from churches of other denominations.

On several occasions, a number of women of different churches asked me to give a series of midweek evening lectures on spiritual healing. Of course I declined for the obvious reason that I was just a beginner; but when they told me that they represented a half-dozen inter-denominational prayer groups all over the city, I had to capitulate to such a demand. To my great surprise, the eight lectures were a success, with an average attendance of sixty.

This convinced me of the need of a healing ministry far beyond the limited scope of a Tuesday morning service. To my knowledge there was no other such ministry in the entire area. It was an opportunity to provide a unique contribution that would enhance the value of an inner-city parish to the entire community. Therefore, I inaugurated the Emmanuel Healing Mission with services every Sunday afternoon at four o'clock. The service is described in detail in the Appendix of this volume.

Advertisements were placed on the church pages of the daily papers every Saturday. A feature article, written by Grace Goulder, in the *Pictorial Magazine* of the Sunday issue of the *Cleveland Plain Dealer,* swelled the attendance to over 200 for a time; some, of course, coming out of simple curiosity. Leaders in the ministry of healing such as the Rev. Alfred W. Price, of St. Stephen's

Church, Philadelphia, and Warden of the Order of St. Luke; Mrs. Emily Gardiner Neal of Pittsburgh; and Dr. William S. Reed, then of Bay City, Michigan, were brought to the Mission to augment my ministry and to keep the interest at a high level. A four-day mission by Brother Mandus of England attracted a total attendance of 2,200. Inspiration and help came from the broadening experience of a three-month tour of Europe for the purpose of attending healing conferences, such as the annual summer Conference of the Guild of Health held at Westfield College of London University, contacting leaders in the field and visiting places of special interest, such as Lourdes. Later I was asked to conduct a Spiritual Healing Pilgrimage to Europe, retracing the steps of the previous tour, with a party of twenty-nine. At that time, I resigned from the active parochial ministry in order to devote myself more fully to writing and speaking on spiritual healing.

All this is added to the story of how I became interested in spiritual healing in order to show the great need for this ministry and the response that comes from an earnest attempt to meet it. Personally, I am deeply grateful for being divinely guided into this work because it has developed my spiritual life, broadened my understanding of the problems people have to face every day, and given me the wholesome satisfaction of trying to help those who are sick in body, mind, and spirit at the point of their need and in the name of Jesus Christ.

God Wants You to Be Well

1.
Man, A Perfect Whole

Cancer linked to the emotions? Impossible, you say. How ridiculous to attempt to relate such a desperate thing as cancer to how one thinks or feels!

Yet utter despair and bleak hopelessness were found in 72 percent of adult cancer patients in a research project carried out over twelve years according to a report given at a Conference on the Psychophysiological Aspects of Cancer held at the New York Academy of Sciences in April, 1965.[1] And at the same conference there was presented a study made over a period of fifteen years on three sets of patients, numbering over one hundred, both men and women, suffering from leukemia and lymphoma, in which it was reported that the disease developed amid conditions of anger, sadness, anxiety, or hopelessness.

Despair. Sadness. Anxiety. Depression. Hopelessness. And you can add to the list many more emotional states that have to be reckoned with, such as guilt, greed, grief,

[1] *Annals* of the New York Academy of Sciences, Vol. 125 (Jan. 21, 1966), Art. 3, pp. 780-800.

envy, frustration, loneliness, and an overweening concern for oneself or for others, with fear being the worst offender.

Yes, all our emotional states are involved in our state of health. If our status is one of happiness and balance, then normality will prevail to maintain health; but if the above negative emotions get out of control and become obsessions, our inward sickness will be reflected in some outward sickness. In nonmedical terms, of course, such emotional imbalance creates abnormal tension, and tension kills, perhaps striking us in some Achilles' heel of an unknown weakness. Where there is dis-ease, there is disease. Lack of appetite or digestive difficulties lower the resistance of the body to infection until we become abnormally susceptible. Too, obsession with inner states may so detract us from our usual alertness to danger that we become prone to accidents.

The medical profession is well acquainted with this psychosomatic approach to both pathology and therapy. That is why we frequently hear or read statements by doctors that so large a percentage of their patients do not really need their medicines or treatments because the sicknesses of so many people are fundamentally self-induced. This fact is illustrated by a four-month survey carried out at the Out-Patient Clinic of the Massachusetts General Hospital which revealed that 80 percent of all the patients had no organic illness related to the symptoms complained of, and that 84 percent had psychiatric problems.

So the sickness of the body can reflect the sickness of the soul, as in the case of that person who complained of her arthritis and suddenly exclaimed, "But mostly it's the bitterness in my heart!" And her self-diagnosis was correct, for doctors have told me that resentment can be a major factor in causing some forms of arthritis. Sometimes one can sense a twisted spirit behind the twisted sinews.

Let it be stated right here, however, that not all our ailments can be traced to psychosomatic causes. Our bodies are mortal. Although created in their several parts beyond our comprehension, yet our bodies are physical and thus subject to all sorts of sicknesses, infection from within and without, as well as to accidents. Because it is mechanical, the body wears out. It will do no good to rebel against this. We accept it as a fact of life. God has made us this way — perhaps to teach us that the body is not all, nor the end of life.

Since God has created us creatures of flesh, He is in that respect responsible for our physical ailments. God does not punish us with sickness. We punish ourselves as we break the laws God has made for our good. God is not on the side of sickness but is on the side of health. He has made us to be well. Built into the structure of our bodies are the restorative and recuperative processes. A common example of this is the presence of the white cells or leucocytes in the blood and lymph, which can kill harmful micro-organisms. It is such a common experience to see a cut finger or a simple infection heal so quickly that we scarcely realize that God's method and power are at work in the process of recovering the wholeness which He created and ordained.

The center of our conception of man being a whole lies in the conception of man being a soul. Neither the manifold experiences of man nor his accumulated wisdom have impoverished, but rather magnified, the meaning of Genesis' ancient word that first of the dust of the earth was man formed and then by the breath of the Creator "Man became a living being" (Genesis 2:7). Body, mind, and soul are so closely interrelated and interdependent that the health or sickness of one affects the other two.

Referring to the emotional states listed above, you will note, if you did not do so at first reading, that most if not all of them represent spiritual problems. How can guilt and grief and fear of death, to mention three of the most virulent, be resolved other than through a therapy of the soul? Spiritual healing is therefore fundamental in the restoration of wholeness because it is the healing of the spirit. Concerning the treatment of the patient as a person and not just as a disease, Dr. Frank J. Sladen, M.D., of the Henry Ford Hospital in Detroit, says that "the miracle of recovery now must be to a state that is better than before the illness. In this wider concept, doctors are now asking patients not only, 'What is your religion?' but, as well, 'What does it mean to you?'"[2]

The recognition of this is taking place in greater measure than most people realize. It is not without significance that today most general hospitals have full-time chaplains in addition to a thorough system for notifying local ministers of the admittance of their parishioners. A new approach to treatment based on actual hospital cases has been given to us by Drs. Richard K. Young and Albert L. Meiburg in their book *Spiritual Therapy*.[3] In this, they relate how the physician, psy-

[2] *Faith at Work* (July-August, 1958), p. 38.
[3] (New York: Harper & Row, 1960).

chiatrist, and minister collaborate at Winston-Salem's North Carolina Baptist Hospital.

Also moving magnificently in this direction is the American Lutheran Church in the establishment of the Lutheran Institute of Human Ecology, which involves a thorough program of interdisciplinary cooperation and treatment. Mr. Frederic M. Norstad, Vice-President and Program Director of the Institute, has written me: "We start with a concept of the person and project into this a program of health care. We view man as an inseparable totality composed of spiritual, physical, mental, emotional and social aspects or factors each in dynamic interaction with the others." Far from being just an ideal, this theory is actually in practice in two of the Institute's hospitals, with two more hospitals soon to open, each using the same procedure. A treatment center for alcoholics and a new hospital to be operated in cooperation with the medical school of a large midwestern university are on the planning boards of the Foundation for Human Ecology.

"No tissue of the human body is wholly removed from the influence of spirit." That statement was actually printed in the *British Medical Journal!* [4] Upon this authority, we need not hesitate to claim that the state of the soul influences the state of the body. Healing must take place at the source. A new pattern of life is required to prevent the same sickness from recurring. I will never forget an address along this line given at a meeting of ministers in Boston by a leading surgeon of that city. He told of a man who came to see him complaining of a

---

[4] Reported in Leslie D. Weatherhead, *Psychology, Religion and Healing* (Rev. ed.; Nashville: Abingdon Press, 1952), p. 40.

stomach ulcer. A little investigation revealed that the patient had made the rounds of doctors and had undergone several operations for the same difficulty besides receiving various treatments, special diets, and so forth. Finally the surgeon said something like this to the man: "Yes, I can operate on your stomach, but you will be back again before too long with another ulcer unless you *change the pattern of your life.* Now I am going to give you a prescription for complete and total healing that I challenge you to follow as seriously as if it were medicine. I want you to have grace before every meal. You are to institute Bible reading and family prayers in your home every day. Have a time of devotional reading and prayer with your wife every night. Take fifteen minutes of your lunch hour for quiet prayer every day. And go to church with your family every Sunday. Will you do it?" The patient, in desperation, agreed — and *it worked!*

As if the pressure of modern business life were not enough of a strain, we increase the likelihood of headaches, ulcers, heart ailments, high blood pressure, and digestive difficulties — to mention only a few ills — through envy of the boss, bickering with the other employees, and perhaps an inner sense of guilt because we are getting by with as little as we can give, and getting away with as much as we can. Recently I read of a large bus line which keeps a close watch on the marital status of its drivers because a man who is having difficulties at home has been found to be more liable to have accidents than the man who is enjoying a happy home life.

At a great Service of Healing in St. Martin's-in-the-Fields, London, the late Dorothy Kerin, founder of a wonderful home of healing called "Burrswood" in Kent,

England, said in her usual saintly way: "Of far greater importance than physical healing is the quickening of the spiritual life within us, the restoration to spiritual health of our souls."[5] And may I give you the illustration of that woman, a former teacher and leader in civic affairs in Cleveland, who came frequently to our services for the laying-on of hands for the relief of failing eyesight? When I inquired about her eyes one day, she replied triumphantly, "Oh, the eyes are about the same, but *I'm* so different!"

Doctors can point the way, we ourselves can help with firm resolve, but the medicine that makes us whole can come only from the One who made us.

> For He Who formed our frame
> Made man a perfect whole,
> And made the body's health depend
> Upon the living soul.[6]

_____
  [5] *The Burrswood Herald,* Vol. 1, No. 9 (June 1965), p. 6. Also Dorothy Musgrave Arnold, *Dorothy Kerin: Called by Christ to Heal* (London: Hodder and Stoughton, 1965), p. 155.
  [6] Jones Very, from "Health of Body Dependent on Soul," in *Poems and Essays* (Boston: Houghton, Mifflin Co., 1886), p. 328.

2.
What Is
Spiritual Healing?

I had forgotten the incident. Then came the letter: "You prayed for the healing of my left arm which had suffered a comminuted fracture of the humerus. Following that service the constant pain left. ... X-ray pictures showed the bone well healed. The doctors say I am most fortunate to have kept the arm. ... I want to share my joy with you, and to witness to God's wonderful love in this remarkable recovery."

What happened? A prayer was answered bringing both healing and renewed faith. A church became a place where God's power came through to bless, and to send forth into the world a person radiant with gratitude. A minister was convinced of a way to revitalize the faith of his people. And once more, a doctor saw the evidence of a healing force at work above and beyond his medications. Call it by whatever name — faith healing, divine healing, the ministry of healing, spiritual healing — there is something happening for us today.

Let us first clear the ground of our thinking by

declaring what spiritual healing is not, before defining what it is.

Spiritual healing is not a substitute for medical care or surgical skill. We believe that the marvelous accomplishments of medical science represent the will of God for our good, through devoted and self-sacrificing men and women who are aware of His divine revelations. We expect that every person who comes to a service of spiritual healing anticipating help for a physical need is under the care of a physician. In every such service, we make it a point to pray for doctors, nurses, and for all who tend the sick in hospitals. We believe in calling the doctor and then praying for him!

Spiritual healing is not an infiltration of Christian Science into the Christian Church. We are grateful that Christian Science filled the void of need when the Christian Church had an empty gospel concerning sickness. We recognize the contribution Christian Science has made in revealing the power of constructive, spiritual thinking in overcoming certain types of illness and in "living above" unavoidable suffering. On the other hand, we do not deny the existence of bodily ailments and death; we believe that Jesus accepted the reality of suffering and, in His compassion, worked to alleviate pain and sorrow by revealing in His healing miracles a power that could overcome disease — a power that could heal the sick, open blind eyes, cleanse leprosy, and make the lame walk.

Spiritual healing is not just positive thinking or mental adjustment, although each of us could benefit thereby. Such a constructive approach with its great affirmations of faith is always helpful in any therapy, but it does not provide the emotional stimulus at the depth we need to change us. When a person is overwhelmed by physical disaster, the advice to think on noble precepts is hardly enough. Christian belief is a bit bland unless it is personified in Jesus Christ. Our faith is not only in great truths but in a saving Person.

Spiritual healing is not just relief from pain, or freedom from a handicap. Unfortunately, the almost universal conception of it is in terms of physical healing at the level of the mysterious and the miraculous, where it becomes a stumbling-block to ministers and an offense to doctors. The therapy we seek must go as deep as the need, which in most cases, is spiritual. If the sickness without is a symptom of the sickness within, then the healing must be at the source, if we are to secure wholeness in body, mind, and spirit. And we always pray earnestly and expectantly that the healing of the spirit will be reflected in the healing of the body.

Then what is spiritual healing? I give three definitions. The first one was propounded by a pioneer and a recognized leader in the field, Dr. Leslie D. Weatherhead: "By healing is meant the process of restoring the broken harmony which prevents personality, at any point of body, mind or spirit, from its perfect functioning in its relevant environment: the body in the material world; the mind in the realm of true ideas; and the spirit in its relationship with God."[1] Second, there is a less psychological and simpler definition attributed to the late Rev. Noel Waring, Canon of the Anglican Cathedral in Dublin, and one who practiced the ministry of healing for many years: "Spiritual healing is God's loving action

[1] *Psychology, Religion and Healing* (Rev. ed.; Nashville: Abingdon Press, 1952), p. 40.

upon all and every part of our nature." Third, I give you my own definition even though it may seem much too simple: "Spiritual healing is the healing of the spirit."

What are you? A body with a soul? Never has a surgeon probing in the body found a soul any more than the Russian cosmonaut found God "up there." No! You are a soul with a physical body by which you are able to exist and express yourself in a physical world. The complex of personality with its body, mind, and spirit is not only dependent upon each of these three facets of its structure, but also subject to their interdependence and interreaction. The condition — the sickness or health — of any one of them affects the other two.

How often we have said with a sigh, "I'm just too tired to think!" Extreme fatigue can so enervate us spiritually that our resistance to temptation is lowered to the yielding point. A dull mind can cause a sluggish body. A soul that is sick from grief or guilt or frustration or just plain loneliness may produce pain as real as if there were a physical ailment.

An old family doctor turned over to his young assistant a woman who had been a patient for many years and who now came complaining of continual dull aching in her stomach. In several days, the young doctor reported to his senior that he had given the patient most exhaustive tests, but could find no physical cause of her pain. When the reports were thoroughly analyzed, the wise old physician remarked, "Do you remember that she lost her husband in a tragic accident several months ago?"

Our main concern is with the soul because it is the center of the personality and the seat of the emotions. It is the source of our feelings and the root of the will. It is what we really are and where we really live. How you feel deep within can make your body sick. Disease in the body may reflect the dis-ease in the spirit. Thus an outward condition can be a symptom of an inward state.

A simple illustration is the common experience of a person blushing when he is ashamed, or blanching white when he is afraid, thus showing how feelings affect even the flow of blood. A more serious problem is encountered when grave emotions, such as anxiety, fear, frustration, disappointment, envy, hatred, hopelessness, jealousy, loneliness, boredom, guilt, and grief are allowed to get out of hand. Thus we become tense. Tension tightens up the body at some point of weakness, often unknown or unsuspected, until a malfunction occurs and sickness ensues. A very close friend of mine has had two oper-ations for tumors which were diagnosed as malignant, and each time the condition followed hard upon a period of excessive anxiety and grief.

No wonder that medical science is aware of the psychosomatic causes of sickness with their psycho-physiological and psychobiological bases! No wonder that physicians are known to declare that 50 percent or 75 percent of their patients do not need their medicines as much as they need religion! Dr. Frank J. Sladen, M.D., of the Henry Ford Hospital in Detroit, has written concerning the "wide-spread recognition of the im-portance of the personality of the individual, his way of thinking, of acting, his very being. Are his actions and reactions such as to help him maintain his health? Or are they an undermining and destructive factor in producing illness?"[2]

---

[2] *Faith at Work* (July-August, 1958), p. 38.

To "blow your top" is a common slang phrase, but I know a man who actually did "blow his top." He was a part-time organist and choir director in a rather small church in a large city. His training was mediocre, his skill below average, and his tactlessness with the choir members so unbearable that scarcely a person remained. Any hint that his work was unsatisfactory caused an explosion of rage. The music committee finally had to take action and voted that he be dismissed, leaving to the minister the task of notifying him. A storm of relentless anger and vituperation broke upon the head of the poor parson. Every Sunday after his dismissal, the former organist sat in the front pew and glared at the minister throughout the service, and the virulence of his tongue knew no bounds. His obsession became so intense that it affected his daily work, and life with him in his home became almost intolerable for his wife and children. As you may have guessed, his temperament was extremely choleric, to put it mildly. Then it happened! In a fit of anger he fell unconscious. The surgeons twice removed portions of his cranium to relieve the pressure. The heavy sedation did not stop his restlessness, and since further surgery was impossible, his wife was told that he would die unless he could be quieted. At that point, the wife and her minister asked me to visit him in the hospital. I have never seen such aggravation in the body of an unconscious person: the face was florid, the muscles twitched constantly, and his entire body was in continual motion. With his tearful wife by my side, I spoke to the patient in low, earnest tones as if he could hear me; then laid on hands and prayed. It was then late evening; sometime during the night he quieted, and in the morning regained consciousness. His restlessness had changed to undisturbed peace; he had passed the crisis. Within a few days he confessed to his wife that his uncontrolled anger and resentment had brought on this critical condition. He asked her to invite their minister to come to the hospital that he might beg forgiveness.

So clearly was his physical near-catastrophe the result of psychosomatic causes that it seems a pity that some person knowledgeable in the matter, like a physician, psychiatrist, or minister could not have warned him what the outcome most probably would be. No doubt his disposition was such that he would have resented any advice or caution. A spiritual healing might well have prevented the climactic consequence. Unfortunately, it would appear that under the circumstances, it was necessary for him to undergo the crucial physical crisis as a means of spiritual healing. Of primary concern, however, was his complete change of heart to the point of realizing that he had allowed his vindictive anger to become the cause of his physical undoing, and then took the initiative in seeking the forgiveness of the man he had hated.

Spiritual healing is the healing of the *spirit!*

Whenever I contemplate that we are souls with bodies rather than bodies with souls, I recall that young man in a state hospital. Some disease had so afflicted his body that he had to lie on his stomach even to eat. A rack had been rigged up so that he could read in that position, and I used to find him going through the Harvard Classics. And there was that other man who was so crippled that his head had to be held up by a strap, yet rubber-tipped sticks were inserted in his gnarled hands so that he could type the poems he composed.

But especially do I think of Jack in my own parish. Big and strong, tall and handsome in his youth, he was so eager to serve in World War I that he joined the Canadian Army and fought in France for four years. In middle life, he was struck with a rare disease that killed the nerves of the blood vessels at his extremities. When I came to know him, both legs had been amputated as far as possible and most of his fingers were but stubs. Even so, he went to his work, being carried to and from a car by devoted friends. He made a low cart on which he propelled himself about the house. For years, he continued as corresponding secretary of his lodge with the special duty of contacting the sick members by telephone. What a spirit! In his presence one forgot his mutilated body. He never let one dare to think of his hopeless condition with nothing in sight but more operations and then death. It was like a tonic to visit him. How he would laugh when he fell out of his cart or got caught in a doorway! He always regaled his visitors with his wit, and his stories were the funniest I've ever heard. Of course there were the times of quiet talk about the deep meanings life held, and always those precious minutes of prayer. His sufferings are over now and his new body is whole. And everyone who had the privilege of knowing Jack is a better person and more able to face valiantly whatever life may bring.

Nearly everyone has had the experience of knowing similar instances even though less dramatic. The resurgent power of the spirit to live above the handicaps of the body is always a wonder to behold. Surely "the phenomenon of man" cannot be explained or understood without seeing behind the facade of whatever condition the body may present, a condition that is greater than the body — something within that makes it possible for a man to overcome his physical handicaps — something that moves the person to wrest a meaningful existence from a seemingly hopeless void.

Spiritual healing is the triumph of the *spirit!*

Little Mrs. A. was as saintly a person as one could ever find. A widow for many years, her interests were her home and her church. Learning that she was ill, I found her in great distress from the aftereffects of a virus cold. While we were conversing, a sudden attack of coughing compelled her to leave the room, and when she finally returned, her weakness was so noticeable that I decided to leave at once that she might rest. At the door, I took her hands in mine and prayed a very simple prayer for her healing. A note from her a few days later tells the story: "For several weeks past on retiring at night, I would have distressing paroxysms of coughing that took my strength and disturbed my rest. The same occurred in the morning and through the day. But that night after your prayer, there was absolutely no sign of a cough and no disturbing symptoms. I slept and rested peacefully. In the morning, no coughing spell occurred, nor have any returned since."

Upon another occasion, she received a healing that was a further revelation of God's love and care. A bad fall had twisted a muscle in her side and the pain and suffering seemed more than she could endure. The doctor who treated her could do little to alleviate the pain and told her that she must be patient and allow nature to take its course. She had lost her courage and become fearful and despondent when she asked for spiritual help. I went to her home and found her almost buried in pillows in a large, overstuffed chair. I folded her trembling hands in mine and asked God to heal her. As we prayed together she frequently winced with pain. A subsequent letter gives her testimony: "That night the distressing pain in my side had completely disappeared, and it did not return again. I was like my old self again. God was with us at the time of this healing touch and prayer, and I am deeply grateful to Him."

I hope that in telling this story, I have made it clear that there was no psychosomatic condition behind her two illnesses. A virus cold and a fall are common exigencies to which our bodies are subject. Her whole being was so full of trust that there was no room for tension. Her heart was so permeated by love that she could understand and accept God's love as expressed in the healing. Her life was enveloped in the love of God and controlled by the Spirit of God.

To the average person these two healings experienced by Mrs. A must seem truly miraculous. The results were both immediate and permanent. There was not the benefit of a healing service in a church with the supporting prayers of other people. The experiences occurred in her home, and the prayers were exceedingly simple. While it is impossible to describe the physical processes that took place, it does seem reasonable to say that her already high level of spirituality was raised to the point at which the healing forces could overcome the debilitating bodily forces. No general conclusions are ever safe in such a religio-physical complex, yet these two examples lead us to assume that spiritual healing can more readily occur in a person of high spiritual attainment. Mrs. A.

had no barriers of doubt or guilt or fear or frustration to overcome. Her faith was translucent and uninhibited. Her experiences of healing were as natural to her as her belief in God. Her days were lived in the circle of the Heavenly Father's love and care. We recall Jesus' words: "If you remain in me, and my words remain in you, then you will ask for anything you wish, and you shall have it" (John 15:7).

Spiritual healing is living in the *spirit!*

3.
The Best Book On Spiritual Healing

"Where can I get a good book on spiritual healing?" is a question frequently asked me. My answer: "Begin with the Bible." It is still the supreme source of inspiration and method if we are to approach this advancing movement from a Christian standpoint.

A broad sweep of thought through the Old Testament reminds us that God is revealed as all-powerful, ever zealous in His purpose, and always mindful of the good of His people. Judgment is His, but His justice is tempered by mercy.

In the Genesis story, God pauses after each creative act to behold what He has done and to declare that it is "good." Never does He deny as evil anything that He has made, and His creation of all things includes His control of all things. The climax of His creation is reached in the making of man as a living soul. All His previous acts are for the good of man looking toward His purpose that man may develop an increasing capacity for the spiritual.

From Moses thundering from Sinai through the succession of prophets stomping into kings' palaces, we see evolving the moral foundations of God's way for His people and the ethical quality of life. When the prophets are burdened with the sins of the people and pronounce certain punishment, they emphasize equally the capacity of God to forgive and to love, thus projecting the prototype of God the Father as revealed by Jesus Christ.

An acute relationship between sin and sickness is found throughout the Old Testament; and it lingers on, with considerable prevalence, to the time of Jesus. The thought was that since God created and controlled all of life, He must have ordained both health and sickness. Divine disfavor meant punishment for sin which resulted in sickness. On the other hand, righteousness brought God's blessing in health and prosperity. Both sickness and health, therefore, reflected the relationship of the person to God, with its effect upon mind and soul. We remember that Job's so-called "comforters" claimed that he was suffering because of his past sins, and when he protested that his life was righteous in God's sight, they doubly condemned him to his suffering because of his hypocrisy.

Although from a different stance today, we are aware of a connection between sin and sickness, especially when a guilt complex is the deep-seated cause of a tension that results in neurosis or sickness. The experience of praying with people and administering the laying-on of hands one by one, has proved the worth of this very personal method in every service of spiritual healing.[1] In a low voice, so that no one else can hear, I inquire the person's

---

[1] See Appendix for a description of the service.

first name. Then I ask, "What shall we pray for?" Quite often the request is for a spiritual need even though there is an obvious physical ailment; and sometimes, sin is divulged and forgiveness sought, so that this becomes the burden of the prayer that follows. In laying on hands upon some others who have not even indicated a spiritual need, I have found myself so sensitive to the real condition that I have prayed that all their sins be forgiven so that holiness may make possible the wholeness they desire. Such an unexpected petition in the prayer has frequently brought such an emotional response that tear-filled eyes of gratitude say the "thank you" because the words cannot be uttered.

Also, the restoration of a right relationship with God through forgiveness represents a therapy more often needed than used. In the healing ministry, the clergyman is frequently called upon to help people who have no church connection. So it was that a telephone message from a stranger sent me to a hospital to see an elderly woman who was also unknown to me. In talking with her during several visits and through conversations with a distant and only relative, I learned that the patient's early church connection had long since been broken and that the years had been wasted spiritually. It was obvious that she had but a short time to live. One day, as the prayer was ended and I was about to leave, she drew me close to hear her whispered plea, "Please tell me about God." Surely it was divine intuition that led me to say, "God loves you!" She looked at the ceiling for a long minute, then with a beatific smile, she turned to her nurse and exclaimed, "Did you hear what he said? 'God loves me! God loves me!'" She was still repeating the words as I left the room. It was the last time that I saw her, but I will never forget the experience — nor that ineffable expression on her face.

The psalms are a superb source of inspiration and help. Only in poetry can there be expressed the mysterious reality of finding God in the midst of life and at the point of our greatest need.

The majestic cadences of Psalm 100 declare our fundamental faith:

> Know that the Lord is God!
> It is he that made us, and we are his;
> we are his people, and the sheep of his pasture.
> Give thanks to him, bless his name!
> For the Lord is good; his steadfast love endures
>   forever,
> and his faithfulness to all generations.

God's answer to man's need is hardly more explicit anywhere than in Psalm 91:

> When he calls to me, I will answer him;
> I will be with him in trouble.

Psalm 116 begins with a paean of love because one of God's children realized His saving help in time of deep trouble:

> I love the Lord, because he has heard
> my voice and my supplications.
> I suffered distress and anguish.
> When I was brought low, he saved me.

The writer of Psalm 38 related a definite connection between his sin and sickness:

> There is no soundness in my flesh because of
> thy indignation

there is no health in my bones because of my
   sin.
My wounds grow foul and fester because of my
   foolishness.

Even so, he has hope because he is sure that God sees
his suffering and will help him:

Lord, all my longing is known to thee,
my sighing is not hidden from thee.

Every prayer for spiritual healing should include the
praise and the thanksgiving of Psalm 103:

Bless the Lord, O my soul,
and forget not all his benefits,
who forgives all your iniquity,
who heals all your diseases,
who redeems your life from the Pit,
who crowns you with steadfast love and
   mercy, . . .

And Psalm 23, "The Shepherd Psalm," is more
familiar and more universally loved than any other. It
finds its way into every sick room, and its gentle phrases
form the prayers of those in distress of body, mind, or
spirit. If spiritual healing is thought of as the healing of
the spirit, what pregnant meaning there is in these words
of sure and proved affirmation: "He restores my soul"!
In the New Testament we find the fundamental basis
of healing as a Christian experience. No less than 58
references are to be found in the Gospels and Acts. That
the ministry of healing was important to Jesus is signified
by the fact that one-seventh of the verses in the Gospels
have to do with His healing miracles and His teaching in
connection with them. To put it another way, one-third of
the verses relating Christ's public ministry are concerned
with His healing miracles. Again and again we read

about the multitudes thronging to Jesus not only to hear His wonderful words of truth, but also to receive His works of love and mercy. It is significant that Jesus points to the Father as the source of both manifestations of power — the words and the works — and declares them to be of equal value as evidence of His Sonship: "The words that I speak unto you I speak not of myself; but the Father that dwelleth in me, he doeth the works. Believe me that I am in the Father, and the Father in me: or else believe me for the very works' sake" (John 14: 10-14).

The variety of methods used by Jesus in His healing miracles is both amazing and confusing. Usually the person receives the blessing in His presence. On other occasions Jesus speaks the word, and the person, even though at some distance, is healed at that moment, thus giving credence to the fact that the power of God's Spirit transcends both time and space. Sometimes He touches the person — even a leper; other times He merely speaks the word of healing. In several instances the pronouncement of forgiveness seems to suffice, indicating that Jesus sees sin as the source of the sickness. This ostensible inconsistency of method is only the divine consistency of adapting the healing power to the need of each individual according to the omniscience which is an attribute of His Sonship. In comparison, our insight must depend upon the rather wooden ways of psychognosis unless we are willing to strive for the deeper intuition that comes through deeper spirituality.

The belief in demons — so prevalent in Bible times — is foreign to modern thought. When His divine intuition revealed possession by an unholy spirit as the cause of distress, Jesus cast out the demon in order to restore wholeness. This power over evil presented undeniable proof to the people that He was more than human. He commanded His disciples to exert this same power, and they, too, cast out demons. I would make bold to prophesy that even in our science-dominated age, we will discover, someday, that possession by earth-bound spirits is a more prevalent cause of sickness in body, mind, and spirit than we are now willing to admit; and that in the not-too-distant future, we will have trained and devout ministers performing exorcisms "in the Name of Jesus Christ."

The laying-on of hands is generally used now in spiritual healing. Often Jesus touched the sick person in the process of healing, and in one instance we read that "he laid His hands on every one of them and healed them" (Luke 4:40). To the command and prophecy of Jesus found in the final verses of Mark — "they will lay their hands on the sick and they will recover" (16:18) — may be attributed in part, the projection of this method into the ministry of the early Church. To touch with the hands is a natural gesture of love. It is not to be considered magical, although we are aware that some persons are born with a sensitivity to suprahuman powers and that this odic force[2] may produce the gift of healing through the hands. In the light of biblical teaching, the

---

[2] The renowned German chemist, Karl von Reichenbach (1788-1869), was the first modern scientist to postulate the existence of a form of energy that seems to permeate all matter, baffling all attempts to control it or to trace its source. He described it as "a current of energy that emanates from certain organic and inorganic bodies, including human bodies, plants, magnets, crystals, and so on." He named the phenomenon "odic force" after the chief god of Norse mythology, Odin, and declared that the force differed from heat, electricity, magnetism, or light. Long neglected by reputable scientists, the theoretical odic force has recently attracted the attention of medical men and others who are interested in the strange powers manifested by gifted spiritual healers. In England, odic force is called radiesthetic energy.

laying-on of hands can mean the impartation of the Holy
Spirit with its resultant healing. It is evident that the
laying-on of hands is not necessary and is not always
used; but in a beautiful way, it does symbolize the
blessing of God and the compassion of Jesus Christ.

Anointing with oil is another method having a biblical
background. We remember that in Old Testament times,
oil was used in blessing, and in the consecration of kings.
While there is no record that Jesus anointed the sick, we
do read in Mark 6:13 that the disciples "anointed with oil
many that were sick, and healed them." In the early
Church, anointing with oil was commonly used in the
ministry to the sick, and this continued into the eighth
century with less and less frequency and with dwindling
belief in its efficacy as a means of healing. Gradually the
nature of the service of anointing was changed into a
ritual for the forgiveness of sins for those who were at the
point of death. In fact, it is noted that about the year 800,
Bishop Theodulph of Orléans issued a proclamation
ordering unction to be used only as a preparation for
death. By the twelfth century, unction had become one of
the seven sacraments of the Church and was used only for
"one who seems to be in danger of death." In 1549, the
Council of Trent ordained that unction "blots out sins, if
any remain to be expiated." When Archbishop Cranmer
compiled the first English Prayer Book in 1549, he
adapted the Visitation Office of the Sarum Manual
including Extreme Unction and the Viaticum — the Holy
Communion given to a dying person or one in danger of
death. However, the present Prayer Book of the Church
of England has excised this medieval form of anointing *in
extremis* and has substituted a brief ritual for the Unction
of the Sick in connection with the service for the

Visitation of the Sick, and this has been followed by the revisers of the Book of Common Prayer of the Episcopal Church in the United States. While this reversion to the biblical usage of anointing as a means of grace looking forward to the recovery and health of the sick thus has been formally adopted, its general use has been severely limited because of its long association with preparation for death. Gradually, however, unction is being redeemed from this lugubrious connection and is being used with the laying-on of hands in spiritual healing, although it is wisely limited, in most cases, to situations affording an opportunity to explain its ancient biblical connotation.

"Is any among you sick? let him call for the elders of the church; and let them pray over him, anointing him with oil in the name of the Lord: And the prayer of faith shall save him that is sick, and the Lord shall raise him up; and if he have committed sins, they shall be forgiven him." These oft-quoted verses from the Epistle of James (5:14-15) provide dramatic insight into the ministry and method of the early Church. In the Acts, we find nine individual miracles of healing by the disciples and apostles, along with seven other references to collective healings. Obviously this is more than a stilted obedience to the command of Jesus. It represents their total response to His continuing presence and to the fulfillment of His promise of the power of the Holy Spirit. It validates their allegiance to their Lord's commission. It proves the divine authority of the Christ they proclaim. So the Gospel is both preached and verified as these men of power go forth to continue their Lord's work in the very midst of a totally hostile world. No wonder the Church grew then as it never has since in its history!

As Jesus Christ is central in the Bible, so He is the

focal point in our approach to spiritual healing. The conviction of His divinity does not lessen His humanity. So much in the Gospels eludes our comprehension; but no one can ever deny Christ's compassion. He cares! His concern is so adorned with sympathy, understanding, thoughtfulness, empathy, that the Incarnation is crowned with majestic gentleness. We can but believe that He is the Son of God because He loves so much the sons of God. Far beyond the duty of obeying His command is the holy privilege of following in the footsteps of the One who leads us as we go and preach and heal in the Name of Jesus Christ.

4.

Why Jesus Healed

"You have a very bad third-degree burn; it will take many dressings and a long time to heal."

Such was the pronouncement of the surgeon to our Miss F. after the teakettle handle had broken, pouring scalding water on her hand. After the dressing had been applied, she came directly to our Tuesday morning service of spiritual healing in Emmanuel Episcopal Church, Cleveland, Ohio, and knelt at the communion rail for the laying-on of hands. I recall distinctly how gently she placed the huge "paw" of bandage in my hands and asked me to pray for the healing of her painful injury.

Exactly one week later, she returned to Dr. K., whose name everyone would recognize, to have the dressing renewed. When he looked at her hand, he called excitedly to his nurse to come to look at the wound over which they had worked only the week before. "Take a good look at it," he said to the nurse, "for this is something we seldom see." Then turning to Miss F., he asked, "What did you do?" She replied that after leaving his office the previous week, she had gone to the healing service at Emmanuel Church, had knelt at the altar rail and placed her hand between the minister's hands, and he had prayed. Dr. K.'s reply was, "Miss F., you have had a miraculous healing! The burn has disappeared entirely. Even the ugly scar I was sure would mark your hand for the rest of your life is not in evidence. When I told you that you would need many dressings, I meant it. Now it will not be necessary for you to come again."

You don't believe it? Written with her healed hand, and dated just eleven days after the doctor had pronounced her wound entirely healed, Miss F. sent me a letter in which she quoted the above statements of the doctor.

Modern man is a blind devotee of science. He does not realize that scientific thought is probably more fluid than that in any other realm of knowledge. Did you ever glance at your old high school textbook on physics? Obedience to certain "laws" of cause and effect is adhered to only until another, higher theory is discovered. "Natural law" is simply the set of theories in vogue at any given time. Advancement in science is accomplished by open minds, able and willing to conceive the possibility of higher laws being discovered that will transcend the theories adhered to at the time.

No room for "miracles?" See that boy there, feasting his eyes upon a picture magazine describing the fantastic achievements of science in the future? He is accepting as "old hat" the things we feasted our eyes upon and thought fantastic when we were young. Any listing of scientific discoveries will be incorrect by the time we have done the addition. The writing of this very paragraph was interrupted in order to watch on television (itself a miracle a short time ago!) the splash-down of Gemini 12 after four days in space, including the longest time a man had spent out of the capsule while in flight. Passing strange that in an age of miracles, we cannot believe in the miraculous!

What is a miracle? In the fourth century, St. Augustine defined a miracle as "an occurrence contrary to what we know of nature." Those who insist that our knowledge is limited to natural law are inclined to resent any interference from the supernatural ("caused by other than the known forces of nature" — Webster's Dictionary), while being forced to admit the presence of a supranatural power. God does not break down natural laws in a so-called miracle: He simply breaks through "what we know of nature" with the operation of laws, new to us, which transcend the old. Applying this to spiritual healing, Dr. Leslie Weatherhead says, "A miracle is a *law-abiding* event by which God accomplishes His redemptive purposes through the release of energies which belong to a plane of being higher than any with which we are normally familiar." [1]

And what about the healing miracles of Jesus? We can, we do, believe in them. We believe in them because we believe in Jesus the Christ of God, rather than that we believe in Him because we believe in the miracles. As Canon Richardson puts it: "The important question is not whether we believe *that* Jesus worked miracles, but whether we believe *in* Jesus as the Lord who has revealed in his mighty acts the hidden secret of his person and his claim upon our lives." [2]

The pendulum of our critical approach to the miracles

---

[1] Leslie D. Weatherhead, *Psychology, Religion and Healing* (Rev. ed.; Nashville: Abingdon Press, 1952), p. 37.

[2] Alan Richardson, *The Gospel and Modern Thought* (New York: Oxford University Press, 1950), p. 92.

of Jesus has swung too far to the left. In the effort to avoid the embarrassment which they cause the modern mind, the miracles have been ruled out variously as the recrudescence of pre-Christian thought-forms, as inter-polations of a later era for allegorical purposes, as myths necessary to augment belief in the divinity of Jesus, or as a method of pronouncement invented by the writers in the desperate attempt to impress the importance of their gospel upon a disbelieving world. Such is only a partial list of the devious arguments advanced by hypercritical exegetes for three-quarters of a century. I have found it easier to accept the miracles of Jesus than the devices used to deny them. One can hardly ignore the historical fact of this aspect of Jesus' ministry without doing damage to His divine stature and to the living heritage of the Gospels, to say nothing of the power of the early Church. Once again, I quote Canon Richardson: "The fact is that all the historical evidence that there is goes to show that Jesus worked miracles, and there is no evidence whatever that he did not. ... Even his enemies ... never tried to argue that his miracles were fakes. ... The one incontestable piece of evidence is that all those contemporaries of Jesus of whom we have any record, friends and foes alike, believed that Jesus worked mira-cles." [3]

A positive, fundamental approach is to consider the importance of the healing miracles. One-seventh of the verses in the four Gospels have to do with Jesus' healing miracles and His teaching connected with them. One-third of His public ministry is in the same category, to put it another way. Did you ever try reading the Gospels, omitting the healing miracles? How emasculated they

[3] *Ibid.*, pp. 98-99.

become! No point or power! And a Christ without compassion! So Illingworth exclaims: "We cannot separate the wonderful life, or the wonderful teaching, from the wonderful works. They involve and interpenetrate and presuppose each other, and form in their insoluble combination one harmonious picture."[4]

A common fallacy is that we can know about the Bible without reading the Bible. All the knowledge we gain from books about the Bible is no adequate substitute for a study of the Holy Word itself. Well might we heed the invitation of St. Augustine: "Let us ask of the miracles themselves what they will tell us about Christ; for if they be but understood, they have a tongue of their own. . . . He was the Word of God; and all the acts of the Word are themselves words for us; they are not as pictures, merely to look at and admire, but as letters which we must seek to read and understand."[5]

The Individual Healing Miracles by Jesus

	Matthew	Mark	Luke	John
A leper whom Jesus touched	8:1-4	1:40-45	5:12-16	
The centurion's servant	8:5-13		7:2-10	
Peter's mother-in-law	8:14-15	1:29-31	4:38-39	
The Gerasene demoniac	8:28-34	5:1-20	8:26-35	
The nobleman's son				4:46-54
The man possessed, in the synagogue		1:21-28	4:31-37	
A paralytic brought by his friends	9:1-8	2:1-12	5:17-26	
Jairus' daughter raised up	9:18-19	5:21-24	8:40-42	
The woman who touched the hem of His garment	9:20-22	5:25-34	8:43-48	
Two blind men	9:27-31			
A man possessed, also dumb	9:32-34			

---

[4] J. R. Illingworth, *Divine Immanence* (New York: The Macmillan Co., 1898), p. 107.

[5] "Tractates on the Gospel of St. John," xxiv, § 2. Translated by Archbishop Richard Trench.

	Matthew	Mark	Luke	John
At the pool of Bethesda				5:2-18
A widow's son raised up			7:11-17	
A man with a withered hand	12:9-14	3:1-6	6:6-11	
A possessed man both blind and dumb	12:22-30		11:14-26	
A deaf man who could not speak plainly		7:32-37		
A blind man at Bethsaida		8:22-26		
A daughter of a Canaanite woman	15:21-28	7:24-30		
The man blind from birth				9:1-14
A woman infirm for eighteen years			13:10-17	
A man with dropsy			14:1-6	
Lazarus raised				11:1-44
A boy afflicted with epilepsy	17:14-21	9:14-19	9:37-43	
Ten lepers cleansed			17:11-19	
Blind Bartimaeus	20:29-34	10:45-52	18:35-43	
After a leper was cleansed			5:14-16	
At Peter's house	8:16-17	1:32-34	4:40-41	
At the time of the Baptist's inquiry	11:2-6		7:18-23	
Near Capernaum	12:15-21	3:7-12	6:17-19	
At Nazareth	13:53-58	6:1-6		
Before the feeding of the four thousand	15:19-31			
Beyond Jordan	19:1-2			
In the Temple	21:14			

In addition there are important testimonies concerning Jesus' healings to be found in Matthew 4:23 and 9:35, Mark 6:56, and especially in Acts 10:38-39, the oft-quoted witness of Peter to the Roman centurion at Caesarea: "How God anointed Jesus of Nazareth with the Holy Ghost and with power: who went about doing good, and healing all that were oppressed of the devil; for God was with him. And we are witnesses of all things which he did both in the land of the Jews, and in Jerusalem; . . ."

As you read the above passages, it was perfectly

natural that you asked the question again and again: *How* did Jesus perform such miracles? If only we knew! Through the knowledge gained from psychology, psychoanalysis, hypnosis, and especially the modern psychosomatic approach to pathology and therapy, there is being revealed great insight into the fundamental causes of certain ailments and the restoration of the person to wholeness of body, mind, and spirit. Yet there is a vast realm of the unknown that can be attributed only to the divine intuition and power manifested by Jesus in these "mighty works."

The diversity of method used by Jesus in His healing miracles is difficult to explain. It is confusing and leads to misinterpretation. As in every discussion, Jesus went to the heart of the matter, and as in every contact with individuals He saw into the depth of each person's motive, so it is reasonable to assume that behind every sufferer He beheld the fundamental cause as well as the need. As we noted before, His seeming inconsistency of method was the divine consistency of treating each person according to his particular need; and as a child of the Heavenly Father, Jesus saw each one as he really was and as he could be. Whether or not there was in His sight a spiritual cause behind each ailment, we cannot say, for the Gospel records are not analytical and we cannot see through His eyes; but we do believe that His healing was both physical and spiritual. Through Jesus the restoration was to complete wholeness of body, mind, and spirit.

Jesus' power to heal came from God. Again and again Jesus refused to claim it as His own apart from the Father. "I tell you the truth: the Son does nothing on his own; he does only what he sees his Father doing. What

the Father does, the Son also does" (John 5:19). This
revealed the Incarnation — His Sonship, His Christ-
hood! It also revealed His oneness in relation to the
Father as well as His perfect obedience to the Father's
will. "The Father and I are one. . . . I always do what
pleases him" (John 10:30; 8:29).

The more important question is: *Why* did Jesus heal?

1. *To prove that He was the Messiah — the One who
was to come!*

The most definite and significant pronouncement of
His Messiahship was made in His hometown of Nazareth. There in the synagogue on the Sabbath, He read
from the prophet Isaiah:

> The Spirit of the Lord is upon me.
> He has anointed me to preach the Good News
>   to the poor,
> He has sent me to proclaim liberty to the
>   captives,
> And recovery of sight to the blind,
> To set free the oppressed,
> To announce the year when the Lord will save
>   his people!

He began speaking to them: "This passage of
scripture has come true today, as you heard it being
read (Luke 4:18-19, 21; cf. Matt. 13:53 - 58; Mark 6:
1-6a).

Of hardly less importance is the incident of John the
Baptist's inquiry through his own disciples, who asked of
Jesus: Tell us, are you the one John said was going to
come, or should we expect someone else?" Jesus answered: "Go back and tell John what you are hearing and
seeing: the blind can see, the lame can walk, the lepers
are made clean, the deaf hear, the dead are raised to life,
and the Good News is preached to the poor. How happy

is he who has no doubts about me!" (Matt. 11:3-6).

It is to be noted that in reading from Isaiah, Jesus selected a passage that prophesied a messiah who would combine proclamations of truth with practical applications of healing power. The answer to the impertinent question of the Baptist's emissaries was given in terms of the "mighty works" He was then engaged in performing, with the one exception of the preaching of good tidings to the poor. As Canon Richardson assures us, "There can be no doubt at all that Jesus saw in his mighty works the signs or proofs that he was the true Messiah of Israel."[6]

2. *To reveal the loving nature of God and the availability of His power to heal.*

The prophecy of a savior who was to come included the idea of one who would save Israel from her sins as well as the political overtone of restoration of the people as a nation. The eventual fulfillment, however, involved a personal redemption. God's providence and purpose had to be expressed in an Incarnation that met, in token at least, a world of suffering, especially when so much of the suffering was attributed to satanic forces. Speaking of Jesus in terms of Jewish hope and prophecy, George A. Buttrick refers to Him as "Judge and Savior and King." And then he adds: "But he gave to these titles a new, deep meaning: the saviorhood was no mere deliverance of the nation from bondage to the oppressor, but a re-creation of human nature; and the kingship was rooted in divine compassion."[7] When Jesus made His pronouncement at Nazareth, He chose to read a prophecy that included a personal ministry of healing as one attribute of the

---

[6] Richardson, *op. cit.,* p. 90.

[7] George A. Buttrick, in *The Interpreter's Bible,* Vol. 7 (Nashville: Abingdon Press, 1951), p. 254.

expected Messiah. Jesus' reply to the question proposed by John's disciples was that they report what they had seen and heard as sufficient evidence that He was doing the intended work of God. In the total view of Jesus' life and teaching and ministry, we call Him Savior because He constantly used that power bestowed upon Him to alleviate human suffering on a personal basis. It is more than just a curious fact that in the Greek language of New Testament times, the word used for "savior" was *soter,* which in common parlance meant "a preserver from hurt and ills." And throughout Wycliffe's translation of the Bible, the world "health" is used for salvation *(soteria).* There is no record or even intimation anywhere that Jesus ever failed or refused to heal those who came or were brought to Him. Throughout the Gospels the lovingkindness of the Father flows like a river of loving power from the hands of the Son. As Dr. Weatherhead summarizes it so well: "The motive of Christ's miracles was in harmony with all His other motives, and one with His love for God and love for men, His trust in God and His desire for man's well-being."[8]

3. *To support His words and vindicate His authority.*

If Jesus had come with only the truths He spoke, He would have been put down in history as the world's greatest teacher concerning God and man. If Jesus had come with only the miracles He wrought, He would have been put down in history as the world's greatest wonder-worker. But when His life and ministry combined both teaching and miracles in supreme, spiritual self-giving with a coherency of purpose and an identifiable goal, Jesus became recognized as the perfect Incarnation of the

---

[8]Weatherhead, p. 36.

living God and the worthy Son of the Father. To prove the point, try reading the Gospels, first omitting the miracles, then the teachings. You will find that the teachings alone lack application, and the miracles alone lack explanation. The Gospels record that the people came to hear Jesus *and* to have their sick ones healed. It is impossible to divorce the two or to attempt to establish the importance of one over the other. Evidently Jesus considered the two manifestations of His authority as equal avenues to faith in Him. Hear His answer to Philip's question: "Do you not believe, Philip, that I am in the Father and the Father is in me? The words that I have spoken to you do not come from me. The Father, who remains in me, does his own works. Believe me that I am in the Father and the Father is in me. If not, believe because of these works" (John 14:10b-11).

4. *To illustrate and demonstrate the nature and meaning of the Kingdom.*

Even a cursory reading of the Gospels assures us of the primacy of the Kingdom in the teaching of Jesus. Many of the parables are in this category. Whether the idea of the Kingdom was understood by His hearers as a given fact of God or as an ideal to be achieved in the future, the reality of the Kingdom was certainly bound up in His person and His power. And Jesus' concern for individual persons defined His own concept of the Kingdom. As Vincent Taylor puts it: "The sovereignty of God in the individual heart and in the lives of men is what Jesus meant by the kingdom. When that rule was a reality, then the kingdom would have come."[9] At once we are reminded of the reply Jesus made to the Pharisees who

[9] *The Interpreter's Bible,* Vol. 7 (Nashville: Abingdon Press, 1951), p. 117.

disputed His authority in casting out demons: "No, it is God's Spirit who gives me the power to drive out demons, which proves that the Kingdom of God has already come upon you" (Matt. 12:28; cf. Luke 11:20). When the devious arguments of biblical criticism have finally ended and the exegetical acrobatics are over, then may we not assume that to both Jesus and His hearers this most significant statement revealed that the visible restoration of the possessed man to sanity was a sign that the Rule of God had taken place — then and there? For this is what happens when the Kingdom is manifested in the lives of persons. In and through His healing miracles, He both pronounced and personalized the Kingdom as the Reign of God overcoming the ruin wrought by sin and Satan. And He made visible in microcosm what the world could be like when all men accept the Rule of God. No doubt this ideal was in Jesus' mind when He included in the prayer He taught us to say: "Thy kingdom come. Thy will be done on earth as it is in heaven." Of this last phrase, one writer claims that it "was the core-thought and deepest desire of Jesus, the well-spring of all His words and actions, the divine obsession driving all creation to oneness with God."[10] If there had been but one healing miracle instead of the many performed by Jesus during His ministry, we would see in that one new, recreated and redeemed person an epitome of the "new heaven and new earth" envisioned in Revelation: "I heard a loud voice speaking from the throne: Now God's home is with men! He will live with them, and they shall be his people. God himself will be with them, and he will

[10] Norman R. Elliot, *How to Be the Lord's Prayer* (Westwood, N.J.: Fleming H. Revell, 1964), p. 79.

be their God. He will wipe away all tears from their eyes. There will be no more death, no more grief, crying, or pain. The old things have disappeared" (Rev. 21:3-4).

5. *To project into the early Church the evangelistic power of a healing ministry.*

Some essential facts that are not to be minimized or missed are that Jesus called twelve men to be His disciples and that He probably devoted much more time to their training than the Gospels indicate. He was concerned that they be fully prepared for the difficult task to which they would be commissioned, and that they not fail. In addition to the private sessions of Master and disciples, they heard the preachings to the multitudes, and debates with the Pharisees, the Sadducees, and the scribes; and also they were witnesses to the healing miracles. They were to learn both from their Master's words and from their Master's mighty works, for soon they would go forth to speak His words and to do His works. As part of their preparation, He sent them out on a trial ministry "to preach the kingdom of God, and to heal the sick" (Luke 9:1-2, 6, 10; cf. Matt. 10:7-8; Mark 6:7, 13, 30). Also, in St. Luke's Gospel, there is the sending forth of the seventy with the same twofold mission (Luke 10:1, 9, 17). Although biblical scholarship regards the end of St. Mark's Gospel as a "supplementary conclusion," since it is not found in the two oldest Greek manuscripts, yet its main injunction is the same dual command, and as the disciples went forth and preached, the Lord confirmed their word by signs and works (Mark 16:9-20). The evidence in the Acts is conclusive, however, for here we have sixteen references to miracles of healing.

The Healing of Individuals

Peter and John heal a lame man at the Beautiful Gate in Jerusalem (Acts 3:4-22)

Ananias heals Paul's blindness at Damascus (Acts 9:10-19, 22:11-13)

Peter heals Aeneas, the paralytic at Lydda (Acts 9:32-35)

Peter raises up Tabitha ("Dorcas" in Greek) at Joppa (Acts 9:36-42)

Peter heals a man crippled from birth, at Lystra (Acts 14:8-11)

Paul frees a fortune-telling girl from a demon at Philippi (Acts 16:16-18)

Paul restores life to Eutychus at Troas (Acts 20:7-12)

Paul is not affected by a snake bite at Melita (Acts 28:1-6)

Paul heals the father of Publius, the chief man at Melita (Acts 28:7-8)

The Healing of Many People

On the Day of Pentecost, by the apostles in Jerusalem (Acts 2:43)

In Jerusalem, by the apostles (Acts 5:12-16)

In Jerusalem, by Stephen (Acts 6:8)

In Samaria, by Philip (Acts 8:5-8)

In Iconium, by Paul and Barnabas, who are called gods (Acts 14:3)

In Ephesus, by Paul (Acts 19:11-12)

In Melita, by Paul (Acts 28:9)

If Jesus had not healed, in all conscience, could He have commanded His disciples to heal? Could the healings have been done "in the name of Jesus" (Acts 3:6; 4:30; 16:18) without reference to the fact that Jesus himself healed? Would their miracles of healing have been recognized as related to the Jesus whom they proclaimed if He had not healed? Is it not reasonable to think that Jesus anticipated the necessity of the power to heal in the ministry of the early Church because He found that power so effective in His own ministry? Canon Alan Richardson gives us an overall answer when he states that "It is impossible to over-emphasize the significance of the healing work of Jesus in the subsequent expansion of Christianity throughout the ancient world and indeed in the whole development of Christian civilization."[11]

Thus we have tried to show why Jesus healed. Without His healing miracles, there would have been an irreparable lack of vitality, power, and persuasiveness in His ministry; and without His continued "works" through the disciples and apostles in the first century, the gospel would have lost its compelling conviction. The fact that Jesus kept His promise that "whoever believes in me will do the works I do — yes, he will do even greater ones, for I am going to the Father" (John 14:12) gave constant assurance that all His promises would be true in His continuing Presence, and especially in the gift of His power to all whose who went forth into the world in His Name.

Because Jesus healed, there is extended into our day a vital faith. The whole Gospel is ours — including the miracles! And the need is even greater than in New Testament times. In spite of the marvelous advances in medical science and technology, our ever-enlarging hospitals cannot keep up with the demand for beds, and our physicians are besieged by patients, many with their self-

---

[11] *The Miracle Stories of the Gospels* (London: SCM Press, 1956), p. 67.

incurred ailments. Monotony, hopelessness, frustration, envy, fear, greed, guilt, grief — these and many other sins of the spirit are taking their toll as the tension they cause eventuates in some kind of physical or mental sickness. No one knows better than the doctor that treatment of the physical symptom is purely palliative unless accompanied by healing within. What a day for the Church to preach the gospel of wholeness and to manifest the power of the Christ who came healing!

We live in an era when many people pray "Thy Kingdom come" with tongue in cheek because they see world conditions speeding toward certain cataclysm, and crime rampant to the point of being out of control. Where is God? What of His power to save the world? If one person could see the power of God save the life of one child, "In the Name of Jesus Christ," then that person could better believe that God has the power to save the world.

From the idea of God stems the idea of life and the world and man. The emptiness of our belief can be traced to our vagueness about God. It is high time that Christians turn again to the New Testament to re-establish their idea of God as the Father of Our Lord Jesus Christ. This will be found not only in the truth that was taught, but also in the evidence of the nature of God as revealed by His power to heal.

The pragmatic test also applies to religion. Does it work? Is it available? Can it grasp hold of our need at the point of life's nettle? Jesus met the sins and sorrows and sicknesses of life head-on, and He did something about them in such a practical way that even the most calloused persons saw in Him a power more than human. Even though they could not comprehend the source of His power to heal, they could not fail to understand His compassion. Jesus never refused to heal anyone who came to Him — and He never failed! Through our belief in this kind of a Savior, we know that God cares.

In the long view of Christianity, Christ's compassion as revealed in the healing miracles has been a dominant factor in the developing altruism of man, giving incentive and inspiration to such concern for others. Call the roll of the great religions of the world, both ancient and modern, and not one of them has produced such considerate mindfulness of the needs of man as has Christianity. This has been, and still is, particularly notable in the relief of human suffering. Because of the manifest compassion of Christ, the adherents to the religion that bears His Name have always been more than believers — they have been inspired to share in the bringing in of the Kingdom of God through the "fellowship of the concerned."

5.

God Wants You to Be Well

"Don't you dare pray for me, padre, I hate God! Look at what he has done to me!"

Less explosively, but with an equal charge of pent-up resentment, the idea of blaming God is more often expressed with sad irony: "The Bible says, 'For the Lord punishes everyone he loves, and whips everyone he accepts as a son' (Heb. 12:6). I just wish he didn't love me so much!'"

Mostly the eyes stare at one, and there is fire in them.

It is human to seek a scapegoat, and God is so handy. Among primitive animists there are strange and awful rites to appease the avenging spirits. Mythology is full of inventions as to why the gods are so vindictive toward man, and of how the heavenly wrath may be thwarted. Buddhism and Hinduism have their karmic philosophy, including the idea that a person may suffer for the sins committed in a previous incarnation. Our Judeo-Christian heritage pictures a God who sends sickness as punishment for sin, even to succeeding generations. The drama of Job was written to refute this idea and to show that even the innocent suffer the sicknesses God sends in order to prove their trust in Him. Both agony and acceptance are found in Job's cry, "Behold, he will slay me; I have no hope; yet I will defend my ways to his face.... I know that I shall be vindicated" (Job. 13:15, 18b).

Still, the idea of sickness as being punishment for sin prevailed in the time of Christ along with the borrowed theory[1] that some ailments could be laid to demon-possession. A curious anomaly existed among ascetic Christians during the first several centuries in the belief that sickness was sent by God to produce holiness on the part of the sufferers and sympathetic generosity in others. With such a pot-pourri before him, the modern man finds it easy to accept one or more of these ideas in his effort to blame a power outside of himself for his sickness.

"It's a cross I have to bear!" is the pious slogan used so often by those who bravely endure their sufferings. In fact such stoics with their noble indifference to pain and their unflinching faith in themselves lend credence to the thought that God sends suffering to make us strong. But can you meet the unrelieved stare of the eyes of a person in the last throes of cancer and believe that God caused such suffering? Or the wide eyes of a beautiful child with leukemia questioning why he can't run and play as do the other children? Or the haunting faces of a young couple who have just been told that their first baby is a

---

[1] See Vernon S. McCasland, *By the Finger of God* (New York: The Macmillan Co., 1951), pp. 74-81.

mongoloid? If God deliberately sends such suffering upon the innocent and the guilty alike, He is not God the Father who sent His Son into the world as the compassionate Christ who came healing.

Perhaps even now, as you read this, you are recalling the innumerable sermons that have been preached and the books that have been written extolling the virtues of patient suffering. Such suffering is God's will, they say. This supine resignation is an offense against all that we know of God and of the human body. However, there is merit in accepting the inevitable so long as we don't blame God and don't refuse to seek every possible means for our healing. Suffering can make saints or produce rebellious sinners. We cannot always control what life brings to us, but we *can* control our attitude toward what life brings. In this, God is on our side.

A famous preacher — I believe it was Harry Emerson Fosdick — described religion as the rubber in a ball: the harder it is thrown down, the higher it bounces. With a real and understanding faith, God can give us the power to overcome, even when conditions within and without do not allow physical healing to take place. Dr. Leslie D. Weatherhead wrote a book on *Why Do Men Suffer?*[2] and dedicated it to his mother and sister "whose bodies were defeated in the battle against painful disease; but who, from that defeat, wrested a spiritual victory which challenged and inspired all who knew them, and made glad the heart of God."

While we have decried blaming God for our ailments, there is the given fact of divine responsibility if we accept God as Creator. He has made us as we are. Like all flesh,

_____
[2](Nashville: Abingdon Press, 1936), p. 5.

our bodies are subject to accident and disease. Physically we are mortal and born to die. Sickness and pain and death are part of our human creaturehood because God has made us this way. Of course we don't like it. Our first reaction is to rebel, which only compounds our suffering with mental anguish. It would be better if we tried to understand the meaning of life. Could it be that God in His infinite wisdom gave us physical bodies in order that we might learn that we are essentially spiritual creatures? Dr. James Martineau, preaching on "The Uncertainties of Life" said, "A world without a contingency or an agony could have no hero and no saint, and enable no son of man to discover that he was a son of God." There is to be found no satisfactory meaning to our existence without a religious interpretation. The purpose of life is greater than the pain of life. Immortality must include mortality even as mortality must include immortality. In *The Letters of John Keats* we read: "Call the World, if you please, 'the Vale of Soul Making'; then you will find our use of the world."

But the other side of the coin shows a more positive picture. The keynote is the psalmist's exclamation: "For thou didst form my inward parts, thou didst knit me together in my mother's womb. I praise thee, for thou art fearful and wonderful. Wonderful are thy works! Thou knowest me right well" (Ps. 139: 13-14). And how the ancient psalmist would have exulted had he known the wonders of the body as we do today! Think of the eyes, the circulation of the blood by the indefatigable heart, the awesome wonder of conception and birth, the complex coordination that makes the body to function as a whole. It is often said that there can be no atheists among doctors. The authoritative word of the great physicist, Sir James Jeans, is equally applicable to the body: "The stream of knowledge is heading towards a non-mechanical reality; the universe begins to look more like a great thought than like a great machine."[3]

And more! God wants you to be well! How do we know? Because He has made us with built-in, automatic powers of healing. Within us are the always-abiding processes of recuperation and restoration with which we cooperate in all healing. God heals. The doctors and the surgeons, with all the marvelous ministrations of medical science, only make possible the work of the healing forces. As the famous French surgeon, Ambroise Paré (1517-1590) declared in the sixteenth century, "God heals the wound; I merely dress it." And a modern doctor describes the healing forces in this picturesque language: "In the body, for example, the necessity for police may arise whenever bacteria enter and infection threatens. As soon as this happens, the police department goes into action, white blood cells are rushed to the spot, and reserve cells are called into action from the bone marrow. Blood vessels are widened so that more blood can be brought to the danger zone. A complex physical and chemical reaction begins whereby substances to combat the bacterial invasion are manufactured quickly — potent bacteria fighters called 'antibodies.' Actually all this takes place a long time before we become conscious that anything untoward has happened. Only when swelling, pain and local redness and heat from increased blood flow attract our attention do we become conscious that something unusual has been going on. Automatically the

---

[3] *The Mysterious Universe* (New York: The Macmillan Co., 1930), p. 158.

body's defense system set all these forces in motion to combat the enemy infection."[4]

Why did God make us with fifty billion white blood cells or leucocytes, as they are called? Is it not because God is truly on the side of health, not of sickness? It is in the divine plan and purpose that we be at our physical best. Did not Jesus say, "I have come in order that they might have life, life in all its fulness" (John 10:10b)? Wholeness of body can make for the fullness of life. In the close interdependence of our nature, a sick body can make a sick soul, even as a sick soul can make a sick body. To be true, there are suffering saints, but they are not saints because they suffer, but in spite of it.

If the Creator has so bulwarked the body against sickness and disease, why do we die? Even the strongest constitution may have some hidden weakness through inheritance. The strain and stress of life may affect a vital organ to the point of malfunction. Accidents to the body may take a greater toll than we realize. The exposure to disease from without can be more than the defensive powers of the body can handle. As the body ages, deterioration in some form seems to take place, and the lack of strength is accompanied by a feeling of tiredness. Everything considered, it is a miracle in itself that the body lasts as long as it does, and that we suffer so little pain.

So even though our bodies are formed of the "dust of the earth" and made to die "according to the flesh," we feel that, just as God wishes us to *be* well, it is also in His loving plan that we die *well!* Is it not a glorious triumph of the spirit to *die* without pain and even without the loss

---

[4] Frank G. Slaughter, M.D., *Medicine for Moderns* (New York: Julian Messner, 1947), p. 11.

of consciousness until the moment that the spirit leaves the body!

In our family circle, there was a grandmother who "died well." At a ripe old age, she finally took to her bed feeling extremely tired, but without any disease and complaining of no pain. The afternoon and evening before her "passing" near midnight, she had talked with animation with the members of the family; and during the last hour, had arisen to sit in her chair. Once she said, "I had hoped to see Will" — a son on his way from a distant state. In a few minutes, those about her knew that she had gone from them. It was a blessed experience for all those gathered about her, and each one wished that he might come to his own earthly end so consciously at peace with himself, his world, and his God. Without the distress of long suffering, she was able to enter the new life in full awareness of that glorious experience. *God wants you to be well! God wants you to die well!*

The assurance that God wants us to be well is enunciated in the statements on Christian healing by several churches in recent years. One of the clearest and most inclusive of such statements is found in the Lambeth Report on the Healing Ministry of the Christian Church: "Health is God's primary will for all His children." The 172nd General Assembly of the United Presbyterian Church received a most exhaustive and detailed Report on the Relation of Christian Faith to Health, which contained this declaration in the Introduction: "It is plainly the understanding of the New Testament that health in body, mind and spirit is the ultimate will of God." More recently, the General Convention of the Episcopal Church adopted unanimously and without debate the most excellent Report of the Joint Commission on the Ministry of Healing (1964), in which these significant sentences occurred: "God does not will sickness. As the Author of good, not evil, He does not cause disease; nor does He willingly afflict His children. (Lamentations 3:33; Matt. 18:14). God wills health and wholeness." That such official pronouncements are understood and accepted today indicates not only a new concept in theology but also a better comprehension of the relationship between sickness and health.

God wants us to be well so that we can fully express ourselves in body, mind, and spirit; for only in the full state of abundant health can we develop our ultimate capacity for creativity that will help move the world forward.

God wants us to be well in order to glorify Him adequately and to proclaim by our abundant health that our bodies are fit temples for the Spirit of God to dwell in. A sick person is not a good advertisement for the Christian religion. The day will come when we will be ashamed to be sick for fear it will be evidence that we have not properly cared for the body God has given us, or that we have deliberately or inadvertently broken some of the laws He has given us to live by.

God wants us to be well in order to achieve His purpose for our existence: to build character and to serve Him. Sickness sometimes leads to self-pity, which is morally dangerous and spiritually degenerative. The strength of good health resembles the asset of armor and sword as we go forth to meet temptation. Jesus said, "Follow me." He was hungry, thirsty, and tired; He suffered agony and death on a cross; but there is no recorded instance of His ever being sick. Throughout the rugged life that was His during that brief ministry, God sustained Him even as He chose Him. When a high and holy purpose dominates our lives, we do not have the time to think about our petty ills, for we are caught up in an eternal adventure. We are serving the great and living God!

6.
Who Needs
to Be Healed?

Hospitals care for the sick. Doctors treat the ill. Spiritual healing is for everybody.

"When I get old and sick and all crippled up, then I'll be interested." How often have I heard that! But why get sick? Why not be healed of the seeds of sickness now? In your garden, do you pull up the weeds as soon as they sprout or wait until they have gone to seed and crowded out the flower seeds you have planted? The source of sickness lies deep in the soil of the soul.

But it is not just the physically ill or old people who need to be healed. It is amazing how responsive young people are to the need for spiritual healing. When I was invited to give a series of addresses on the subject before the entire student body of a college in Ohio, I shuddered at the improbability of interesting college youth. But the reaction was terrific. They listened with more than usual attention. Scores wanted to ask questions. The luncheon-hour forum could hardly be closed in time for scheduled classes. The college radio station wanted a broadcast on the subject. The housemother of a men's dormitory declared that she had never heard so much discussion about a chapel address. And in a mission or a service of spiritual healing, it is not uncommon for young people and members of junior choirs to come forward to receive the laying-on of hands. The Order of St. Luke has set aside a special chaplain for the ministry of healing to children; and "The Junior Page" is a regular feature of its magazine *Sharing*.

The universal need to "unwind" signifies the prevalence of tension in our common life today, and this in spite of the shorter working hours with more time to relax. We recognize that the pace, the drive, the competition, the noise, the confusion, the crowds — all contribute to the tensive quality of life. These exterior influences are not as great, however, as the fact that man does not feel at home with himself or in his world. This prevailing dis-ease expresses itself in the extremes so characteristic of our day. We are an ulcerous generation. We do battle with the world about us because of the pain within, not knowing that the enemy is in ourselves: tension, the greatest killer of our day!

"Emotional stress is, today, our Number One cause of ill health" claims Dr. John A. Schindler, M.D., chairman of the Department of Medicine in the Monroe Clinic, Monroe, Wisconsin, in his popular book on *How to Live 365 Days a Year*.[1] And in his Introduction he boldly states that "over 50% of all the illness that doctors see is emotionally induced illness." His first chapter,

---

[1](Englewood Cliffs, N.J.: Prentice-Hall, 1957), pp. xix, xx, 4.

entitled "Your Emotions Produce Most of Your Physical Disease," contains these two significant findings: "A few years ago the Ochsner Clinic in New Orleans published a paper which stated that 74% of 500 consecutive patients admitted to the department handling gastrointestinal diseases were found to be suffering from EII (emotionally induced illness). And in 1951, a paper from the Yale University Out-Patient Medical Department indicated that 76% of the patients coming to that Clinic were suffering from EII!"

What are some of the common causes of tension and how can spiritual healing help you to overcome them before they make you sick?

Life. Has it got on top of you? Its problems out of hand? Everything against you? People "in your hair"? In a small town a plumber had his shop on the first floor with his living quarters upstairs. On the window of his shop was painted his name and his business, but underneath and to one side were these two words in small letters: LIVING ABOVE. Wherever the power of prayer is seen and felt, whether in a great cathedral or in the privacy of your own house, the things of life fall into their proper places. We sense that God *is* and that God *cares*. As we align ourselves with "the spirit of calm and the central peace of the universe," there can come a new perspective and a greater poise. When we see the Spirit of God working upon the body to lift each sufferer to new life, we envision the supremacy of the soul. Something eternal has come in. We are able to "live above" life.

Frustration. Remember riding on a merry-go-round that kept on going after the music stopped? Suddenly the fun was gone and you got dizzy. It was just a plain, monotonous "go-round" without the "merry." Multitudes are aboard a "go-round." And their patron saint is St. Vitus — just endless activity with the feeling of "beating the air." I was in a hotel barber shop. The man in the chair next to me and his manicurist were having an earnest conversation, but I could hear only snatches of it because my barber kept talking to me. When the man got up to leave, the girl said, "When you find out what it's all about, let me know, will ya?" And he flung back, "Yeah, yeah, if I ever do." Life needs to be shaken down to its reality where we can find God at its center and discover the meaning of existence. A sense of proportion and purpose comes when we see God at work saving a body so that a person can serve Him with new direction and dedication. Zest and vigor always accompany the therapy of spiritual direction, and life becomes worth living again.

Resentment. It is surprising that so many people hold a perpetual grudge against life. Some have the capacity of being constantly bruised by factors beyond their control. Others carry an unhealable hurt through contact with other people who have offended them. Envy, jealousy, and bitterness, are added to the witch's brew. Hatred is the scum on top. A martyr complex is frequently stirred up from the bottom. Defeats are collected as avidly as a boy fills his pockets with agates during the marble season. Offenses are worn proudly like an ever-lengthening string of beads. Resentment makes for tension, and tension makes for sickness. A wise man has said that there ought to be one more Beatitude: "Blessed is the man who doth not collect resentments." But the spirit of resentment dissolves in an atmosphere of love. You cannot hate the person for whom you pray. When you see God's love healing the outward hurt, you know that His love can heal the bruised heart within. In that quiet moment in the healing service[2] when the person considers the question we ask, "What shall we pray for?" the request is often for a new attitude toward others. When we realize how much God cares for all His children, we find it both possible and necessary to accept, in the spirit of love, all with whom we have disagreed. When the healing of the spirit is sought in time, it obviates the necessity of the healing of the body later.

For several Sundays, a woman came to the altar for the laying-on of hands, but was so emotionally upset that she could not respond to the usual question as to the purpose of our prayer. Finally, at the door, I invited her to come to my study to talk about her problem. When she finished talking about her "nerves" and her utter loneliness, she unearthed a dreadful story of resentment against her sister who was her only living relative. Long years of ill-feeling were climaxed in a dispute over their mother's will, harsh words had been spoken, and this one had vowed that she never wanted to see her sister again. "It was so long ago," she said, "and so wrong on my part as I see it now. I've learned through a mutual acquaintance that my sister is quite ill. What if she should die before this awful thing is made right between us? Tell me what to do." I suggested that she write to her, since the sister lived in another part of the country, and ask if she might visit her at the earliest opportunity. She doubted that the letter would be answered or even

---

[2] See Appendix.

opened. However, she finally said that she would write. Then we went into the chapel to pray for forgiveness, and for the health of the sister, and for a definite reconciliation. It was an entirely different person who came into my study two weeks later, exclaiming, "It worked! My sister is much improved, and I'm to be with her at Christmas time! May we go into the chapel again to thank God for His help?"

Fear. Everybody is afraid of something, and the secret fears are the most virulent. Our apprehensions are so manifold and are so often the deep-lying cause of tension, that a later chapter (chap. 7) is devoted to the treatment of this subject. Spiritual healing brings us to a new concept of God in which our fears are transcended by trust.

When the past has caught up with you. Psychoanalysis and hypnosis have developed techniques for laying bare our past. Traumatic experiences, sometimes long forgotten, are brought to the surface and recognized as the culprits which cause a serious mental or physical sickness. A woman kept coming to our services of spiritual healing. She was obviously a sick person and asked for healing for her "nerves." Noting that she seemed to be deeply troubled, I asked if she would like to talk a bit about her problem. She accepted the suggestion eagerly, and made arrangements to come from her distant home the following week. What a story she poured forth! There had been several operations and her doctor had her on a continuous program of pills for her heart and for insomnia and for what she described generally as "nerves." She said she never went anywhere and had no friends. She was on the "outs" with her neighbors and every relative had offended her in some way. The marital relationship had developed to the point that she and her husband had not spoken a word to each other for months although they continued to live in the same house. During her lengthy recital of this pitiful story, she kept saying, "Oh, I'm so fearful!" Finally I looked at her intently and put the question, "What are you afraid of?" She looked away and was silent for long minutes. Then tears welled up in her eyes, and through quivering lips, she whispered, "Death!" At first she said that she didn't know why, but that she had always been afraid of death and everything connected with it. When I pressed her to try to think of some experience, perhaps in early childhood, that might have been the cause, slowly she revealed this story. As a child, she lived next door to her uncle's furniture store which was combined with an undertaking business, as was customary in small, isolated towns. Above the store was a shop where they made coffins. She and her cousins liked to play up there, braiding the long shavings and making kites of the slender sticks. One day, just for something new to do, they put her into one of the coffins and slammed down the lid and ran off, leaving her to kick and scream in her terror. Fortunately, the lid did not fasten, and she was able to get out and run home. The experience haunted her for days, and her nights were filled with terrifying nightmares about it. Now in middle life, the long-forgotten incident had borne its evil fruit to ruin her health and happiness. It is quite significant that Agnes Sanford frequently asks the sick and troubled people who come to her if they had a happy childhood, and also makes it a point in her Missions to beseech her hearers to ask for cleansing and forgiveness for the past years, recalling a decade at a time. We should never underestimate the damage that comes from the evil things that have lain dormant but alive, "eating us" through long years. When we say that spiritual healing is the healing of the spirit, we include the awareness that wells up to reveal a haunting past and the Grace that understands, cleanses, and overcomes.

Sin. Dis-ease indicates primarily a wrong relationship with God. This causes us to be uncomfortable in the company of others, except perhaps our boon companions, for fear we will be found to be less than they think we are. And a guilt complex with its disturbing dissatisfaction with ourselves produces an inner state of being that gnaws at the vitals of both mind and body. How desperately true are the words of the General Confession: "We have erred, and strayed from thy ways like lost sheep . . . . We have followed too much the devices and desires of our own hearts. We have offended against thy holy laws. We have left undone those things which we ought to have done; and we have done those things which we ought not to have done; and there is no health in us." When we come face to face with the reality of God, we come face to face with the reality of ourselves. This often happens in a service of spiritual healing. The physical need is eclipsed by the spiritual need. During a certain Mission, it seemed that all who were so inclined had come forward for the laying-on of hands, and I was about to close the service. Yet something made me hesitate, and once more, I gave the gesture of invitation. To my great surprise, the organist came down and knelt at the communion rail. He was a handsome young man who gave every evidence of perfect health. When I asked him:

"What shall we pray for?" he lifted his tear-lined face and whispered, "That my heart and mind may be pure."

Also, there are those who do not feel a need themselves, but who come to a service of spiritual healing to expend their strength and conviction in prayer for others. Their prayer-power is unmistakable and very real. They are given a vital opportunity to participate, for everyone present is requested to pray for each person who comes forward as hands are laid upon him. Sometimes the billowing force of prayer from the congregation is overwhelming in its spiritual power.

Then there are others who come to pray for a dear one who is ill at home or in a hospital. Often this is like a pilgrimage of faith, for which they may travel many miles. The names of those whom they represent are sent to the altar to be read aloud and repeated by the congregation during the service. Occasionally a person feels so close to the ill one or has him in such immediate concern that he comes forward to make his prayer of intercession with the missioner or leader. Children do this in a touchingly simple way, asking that we pray for a sick brother or sister, a father or mother, or even for a favorite old aunt or grandparent who has already become the victim of the degenerative acids of age.

Spiritual healing is more than a religious method to cure the sicknesses of body, mind, and spirit. Spiritual healing is *a way of life*. It is an attitude that heals before the hurt comes. It is an awareness of the potential danger involved in the causes of disharmony in every personal and social relationship. It is a conviction that God's Spirit is the power that can and must be accepted to produce poise and peace in every situation; for there is no problem of *any* nature which cannot be healed by the Power of the Spirit. Whether it be a marital problem or difficulties in bringing up children or misunderstanding with fellow workers or discord in a social group or a factious spirit in a church, we know that dissension means dis-ease and the resulting tension causes sickness. Empathy is an antidote for ill-feeling. Forgiveness purifies the emotions. Love marks the highway to health.

Spiritual healing is for everybody!

7.

Watch Out
for Your Fears

"When your knees knock together, kneel on them!"
— Sign in front of a church in London during the blitz

What can you learn about life from fifty thousand letters? When the late Rev. Dr. Joseph Fort Newton was the rector of the Church of St. Luke and the Epiphany in Philadelphia, he wrote a daily column for the *Philadelphia Daily Inquirer*. During the first six years, he received fifty thousand letters in response to his dealing with the common problems of life. Commenting upon this experience, he said: "I learned that the greatest obsession which bears down upon man is fear."

Watch out for your fears! They have an uncanny way of catching up with you. Twenty-five hundred years ago, a very wise man put these words into the mouth of Job (3:25):

The thing that I fear comes upn me,
and what I dread befalls me.

Never underestimate the importance of fear! Fear is
universal. Fear is a natural instinct. Dr. Samuel Johnson
said long ago, "Fear is implanted in us as a preservative
from evil." Fear is a necessary and educative part of our
make-up. What pains we take to train children to fear
certain dangers that would cause serious harm, such as
fire, falling, or busy street traffic! Fear is an automatic
reaction to danger that warns us to protect ourselves.
Henry Ward Beecher put it descriptively: "Fear is a kind
of bell or gong which rings the mind into quick life and
avoidance upon the approach of danger." Fear makes us
prudent. Without fear, we would be fools!

But we are now concerned with the problems of life
that come to us *when the fear of life exceeds the trust of
life,* for when fear gets out of hand, we become victims of
chronic anxiety. And fear is the most common and the
most subtle of all the emotions experienced by man. A
technical dictionary defines fear as "an emotion of
violent agitation or fright in the presence (actual or
anticipated) of danger or pain. It is marked by extensive
organic changes."[1] Fear affects our bodies. Dr. Robert
W. White of Harvard University testifies that "gastric
motility, secretion of gastric juices, and peristaltic move-
ments of the intestine are all inhibited by the sympathetic
discharges that go with fear."[2] Fear produces the extra
glandular secretions to give our muscles the power to
fight the impending danger or to flee from it. Such extra

---

[1]Horace B. English and Ava C. English, comp., *A Comprehensive
Dictionary of Psychological and Psychoanalytical Terms* (New
York: Longmans, Green and Co., Inc., 1958), p. 204.

[2]Robert W. White, *The Abnormal Personality* (New York:
Ronald Press, 1948), p. 429.

strength given to the muscles at a time of danger borders on the superhuman. The fatal fire on the USS *Oriskany,* a carrier in the Bay of Tonkin off North Vietnam, would have been a much greater disaster had it not been for a handful of young sailors. They dared the intense, white heat of the burning flares to get several hundred bombs away from the blaze. The 500-pound bombs were usually handled by four men, but under the stress of *fear,* two men carried the bombs and threw them over the side of the ship, never thinking of the weight. Afterward they did not know how they were able to do it.

Imaginary fears produce the same results without providing an outlet for the pent-up strength. Tension results. The digestion is disturbed, the heart races, the muscles become tense, and even the resistance to germs is lowered. Fear can counteract the skillful hand of the surgeon and make the simplest operation a dangerous one. The fear of sickness prepares the ground for sickness. There is the ancient story from the Orient that tells of a ruler who passed Cholera riding fast on a camel. "Where to this time?" the ruler called out. "To Bagdad where I'll kill twenty thousand," came the reply. When they met on their return journey, the ruler accosted Cholera, "You lied. You killed a hundred thousand!" "You're quite mistaken," Cholera answered. "I kept my promise. I killed twenty thousand. Fear killed the rest."

Fear is described as the most disintegrating enemy of personality. It causes worry and an inferiority complex. It includes pessimism and uncontrollable greed. Sleepless nights occur through dread of the anticipated calamities of the next day. Fear makes us cowards before the problems and responsibilities of life. Job was right.

The thing that I fear comes upon me,
and what I dread befalls me.

Some people develop an abnormal fear of sickness.
They have an obsession about their physical condition —
imaginary pains and an overapprehensive concern about
their health that makes every trivial upset a sure symptom of some fatal disease. Fear aggravates the hidden
wish to die. Fear generates a fear of fear itself until we
are afraid of being afraid and we become victims of
phobophobia. Fear kills. It is possible to be scared to
death. Or we can be scared stiff. Fear paralyzes our
bodies, stops our thinking, and short-circuits our spiritual life.

Everyone is afraid of something, either admitted or
unconfessed. Some fears have been brought out into the
open and recognized for their universality, as well as the
damage they do. There is the fear of any unsettling
situation that may make us less sure of ourselves; a rut is
so comfortable, after all! And what if we should be
exposed for the person we really are? Then there might
come disregard or humiliation or ridicule. Some find it
unbearable to contemplate any change within or without.
The fear of failure makes us inadequate to meet the tests
of life; the fear of poverty keeps us poor; the fear of
people fends off those who would be our friends; the fear
of dying fills every living hour with the haunt of death.
Add to these scores of others, like the fear of old age, the
fear of the dark — as well as your own pet fears.

What shall we do about our fears?

Instead of denying them, or hiding them, or running
away from them, why not face our fears to see what they
really are? Let me tell you of an incident that happened to

my father when he was a young man. Coming home late one night, he had to pass an open field. Suddenly he heard steps behind him. They came nearer and nearer. Heavy breathing was upon his back. He would not run, but he walked as fast as he could. He decided that at that next tree, he would turn and face his attacker. When he whirled around, he was smacked in the face — by the cold nose of a cow! Poor, lonesome bossy! She had got loose from her chain, and, tired of wandering about, thought she'd follow the friendly man who came along just then.

Direct action is recommended as a most effective remedy, too. A man came to me for counseling one day. After describing his physical condition, he went on to disclose his fears. There seemed to be nothing that he was not afraid of, from the possibility of an operation to the probability of a traffic accident, although he drove his car so slowly on the city streets that he himself was a hazard to other drivers! One thing I remember particularly is that he shaved himself with a straight razor but was so fearful that he would awaken in the night and slash someone in the house that he kept his razor in another room; and he was so afraid of cutting his throat with it that he would not shave unless someone was nearby. If this pictures him as a hopeless neurotic or a "queer" person, let me quickly add that he was a most engaging personality, attractive in every way, very sociable and a brilliant conversationalist — but filled with fear. He was a bachelor and frequently spoke of his deceased mother. In fact, he readily admitted her dominance over his life, especially since he was her only child. When he told me of the number of pictures of her which were all about the house, I thought I had a clue to his obsessive fear. I dared him to pack them all away — which he finally got the courage to do. It was amazing how soon he was able to overcome his fears, even that of the razor. He was fond of travel, but the very thought of being in a plane made him sick. After the pictures had been hidden and the other fears resolved, he actually flew to New York, and then to Europe, testifying later that he enjoyed every minute of the trip — after the plane got off the ground! You see, if you handle your fears one by one with decisiveness and courage, you will find that they will shrivel into less significance. You will be the master over them. You will be free. How wise were Emerson's words: "He has not learned the lesson of life who does not every day surmount a fear."

The cure for fear is Faith. In terms of Christian belief, how can we put our religion to work to conquer our fears?

1. *Live a good life.* This sounds terribly preachy, but it is an unalterable fact that at the center of our religious life lies plain, honest morality according to the precepts of Christian truth. All our theology, all our worship, all our church activity cannot take the place of the good life. Most of our fears can be traced to our sins: the things we've done that we shouldn't have done and the things we should have done that we haven't done! The more we move away from God, the more we become afraid of God, and the fear of God's judgment is the cause of most of our fears. "Thus conscience does make cowards of us all."

2. *Go to church.* There you will find fellowship with the fearless. You will sing the great hymns of faith. You will hear from the Bible the timeless stories of God's

heroes. You will hear from the pulpit the gospel of the triumphant Christ. You will strike hands with the Christian martyrs. You will go out with the conviction that a vital, living faith in Jesus Christ can conquer all things — even death itself. While fighting through Brittany in World War II, some American soldiers saw an inscription over the door of a bombed-out monastery. It was in Latin and when translated, had this message for them: "Fear knocked on the door. Faith answered, and no one was there." Truly, faith and fear cannot be in the same place or in the same heart at the same time.

3. *Get hold of some great affirmations.* Put them on your desk, your mirror, or over the kitchen sink. Keep them in your mind. Repeat them at every odd moment during the day. Say them over and over before you go to sleep. You know many to use, but may I give you some suggestions:

The Lord is my shepherd (Ps. 23:1).

When I am afraid, I put my trust in thee (Ps. 56:3).

I sought the Lord, and he answered me, and delivered me from all my fears (Ps. 34:4).

The world will make you suffer. But be brave! I have defeated the world (John 16: 33b).

For the Spirit that God has given us does not make us timid; instead, his Spirit fills us with power and love and self-control (II Tim. 1:7).

In his *Prescription for Anxiety,*[3] Dr. Leslie D. Weatherhead tells a story related to him by Hugh Redwood.

---

[3](London: Hodder and Stoughton, 1956), p. 110.

The great journalist from London was staying at a friend's house before giving an important address. He arrived very tired and under the strain of impending decisions. His host was thoughtful enough to escort him to a quiet room upstairs away from the chatter of other guests. There Redwood slumped into an easy chair before a cheerful fire. Then he noticed an open Bible on a table at his elbow. Before him was Psalm 59, and the 10th verse read: "My God in his steadfast love will meet me." But someone had penciled this interpretation in the margin, "My God in His loving kindness shall meet me at every corner."

4. *Learn to trust God as much as you believe in Him.* Let your faith grow into assurance. Put your fears into God's hands — and leave them there! His care of us yesterday gives us faith for today.

> We thank Thee for the yesterdays that have
>   given us reason for faith,
> And the todays that now claim us in our trust,
> We give over the anxieties of tomorrow with
>   their uncertainties and unchartered roads.
> The faith of today gives us confidence,
> And the trust of yesterday makes us bold
> To walk with heads high and courage strong.
> Eternal God, we feel we are Thine and a part of
>   Thee;
> As the child trusts its parent,
> As the bird trusts the air, and the wild thing its
>   sure instinct,
> So we trust Thee and Thy creative effort within
>   us. [4]

---

[4] From "A Prayer Concerning Faith" in Russell L. Dicks, *Toward Health and Wholeness* (New York: The Macmillan Co., 1960), p. 28.

One of the most popular preachers in America once told of his first flight in a small plane. He was on a speaking tour and had to get to another city for a big evening meeting as soon as he could get away from a luncheon meeting. Hurrying to the airport, he found that the flight had been canceled. There was no other flight to that city and no train service that would get him there in time. In desperation, he finally persuaded a private planeowner to take him to the other city. The little machine wobbled and roared down the runway, and, when at last it got into the air, it seemed to be at the mercy of the gusty wind that was blowing, for it tipped and swerved and shuddered at every blast. The preacher was really scared. He hung on for dear life. He knew they'd never make it. He could hear the chairman announcing, with deep regret, that the speaker for that evening had died in a plane crash. Suddenly he looked over at the pilot. His face was calm and confident. His hands were firm but relaxed on the stick. He gave every assurance that his little ship would make it safely. As long as he looked at the pilot instead of the waving treetops just below, the passenger's fear was transformed into trust.

8.

Do You Really
Want to Be Healed?

What a question to ask! Who doesn't want to be healed — to be relieved of suffering — to be freed from a handicap?

But not everyone really wants to be healed, unbelievable as it may seem. The perverseness of human nature makes the desire somewhat less than universal. So easily do we grow accustomed to a certain pattern of life that the edge of effort becomes dull. We resent being raised out of the rut of a routine. A prolonged stay in a hospital may bring on "hospitalitis." Patients have been known to object to the hard work of the therapy necessary to develop their physical capabilities. Chronic invalids find it comfortable to accept the tender care with which they are often enveloped, until their state is fixed and confirmed forever.

The English physician W. L. Northridge, trained counselor and well-known lecturer on the relation of religion and mental health, tells of a patient who was finally persuaded to attend a service of healing, but when the minister was about to lay on hands for her healing, "she found herself praying that she might not get well." And he adds, "She was getting too much satisfaction out of her illness to want to be healed, and to be without this illness would very greatly impoverish her emotional life. . . . Many people who go to faith-healing meetings to be healed, do not really want the healing. This is true of all who suffer from the symptoms of hysteria, which is a purposive illness."[1]

The mind-set against getting well may represent a syndrome of spiritual degeneration. A person who has been "hurt" by life through undeserved criticism, ostracism, alienation, or extreme disappointment may be inclined to enjoy an inordinate satisfaction in the attention now heaped upon him. In an acute state, such an attitude may lead to some form of retributive vindication to the extreme point of actually making oneself sick in order to get sympathy or to take a twisted form of revenge on others by causing them trouble and sorrow.

Ulcerative colitis is a disease of the large intestine that is generally considered to have psychosomatic origins; in other words, emotional conflicts in certain people may be expressed in physical changes in the lining of the large intestine. When my son was in his residency, there was a teen-age boy in the hospital who was afflicted with ulcerative colitis. In that case, the relationship between emotional conflict and physical condition was striking. Every time the boy's mother visited him, the physical condition became much worse, despite vigorous medical

---

[1] W. L. Northridge, *Disorders of the Emotional and Spiritual Life* (London: Epworth, 1960), pp. 91, 123.

treatment. Even though the physicians limited the mother's visits more and more as her son's condition deteriorated, the boy eventually died. It seemed that the emotional conflicts between mother and son could be ended only with the boy's death.

A more common form of neurosis is the use of "invalidism" as an easy escape from life. To get well would necessitate the acceptance of responsibility — to do house-work again or to go back to the job. Dr. Weatherhead relates[2] that he was told by a famous surgeon about a woman whose sickness was diagnosed as inoperable cancer. A few days later he gladly informed her that the tests proved that a mistake had been made and that she could go home, to which she replied, "I cannot bear the thought of facing life again."

This strange quirk in human nature is not new. Jesus found it in healing the man who didn't want to get well (John 5:1-15). It was at the Pool of Bethesda in Jerusalem where, on the five porches surrounding the water, lay the sick waiting for the bubbling of the water; for, according to the belief of the people, this phenomenon was accomplished by an unseen angel, and the first person to step into the "troubled" water would be healed. Jesus sought out a man who had been there thirty-eight years, and asked him, "Do you want to get well?" The answer was a whine. "Sir, I don't have anyone here to put me in the pool when the water is stirred up; while I am trying to get in, somebody else gets there first" (John 5:6c-7). Cannot we assume that his family and his friends had been there in turn to help him at the beginning of his

[2] *Psychology, Religion and Healing* (Rev. ed.; Nashville: Abingdon Press, 1952), pp. 47-48.

sickness? And when they were worn out by his complaining, there must have been kindly people of the city
who were attracted to this place in order to help the
unfortunates who had no one else to aid them. Even they
must have grown weary of his peevish fault-finding.
Thirty-eight years of that! What a pitiful creature he
must have been! No wonder Jesus sought him out. And
he expected Jesus to help him to be the first one into the
water after the next "troubling." But the Great Physician
saw that the man needed more than he thought he
needed. The sickness had now become a neurotic mind-
set that required drastic action. "Get up," said Jesus,
"pick up your mat and walk!" (John 5:8). The command
shocked him into obedience. Later, Jesus saw the man in
the Temple, still carrying his pallet, even though it was
the Sabbath day when such burden-bearing was unlawful.
Jesus said to him, "Look, you are well now. Quit your
sins, or something worse may happen to you" (John
5:14).

How does a person get over the sickness of not wanting
to get well?

It is a sin to harm the body, the "temple of the soul,"
by conscious acts of omission as well as by overt acts of
damage or destruction. It is also a sin to run away from
life. The first step in overcoming any sin is *confession*.
This requires perfect honesty. It is to take a long, hard
look at oneself with candid judgment, unmixed with self-
pity. It is to recognize the moral dangers of this common
form of egotism. It is to see self-centeredness as sin.
Contrary to popular opinion, sickness itself does not
necessarily make for goodness any more than imprisonment. It may only limit our activity for a time. Our high

resolves may be the result of discomfort or fear rather than a sincere desire to be a better person. In fact, sickness may unmask our true nature. Putting ourselves in the hands of God removes the block that prevents the Father's light and love from flowing in. It is His will that we become both whole and holy, and in the deepest sense, we cannot be one without the other.

Confession includes, in the same breath, the plea for *forgiveness*. The age-long story of the relation of God to man and of man to God as told in the Bible is replete with instances of divine grace. Simply and humbly and with complete confidence we ask God to forgive us in the assurance that "if we confess our sins to God, we can trust him, for he does what is right — he will forgive us our sins and make us clean from all our wrongdoing" (1 John 1:9). If our self-centeredness has offended or done any injustice to those caring for us, then we are obligated to ask their forgiveness, too. This is not easy, for it hurts our pride, but it is always a sign of strength rather than of weakness. Nobility awakens nobility. Your confidence will be strengthened by greater respect.

"But I just can't forgive myself!" How often have I heard that! Yet morbid remorse will cause inner tension to the extent of hindering the healing process. If God in His mercy has shown His love in forgiveness and if others have responded with true magnanimity, can you not believe that your own sincerity will strengthen you to let the matter go? I admit that this process of forgiving oneself is not easy, but the joy that awaits its accomplishment is greater than the pain of regret. As Pompilia said:

There seems not so much pain.

It comes most like that I am just absolved,
Purged of the Past; the foul in me washed fair. [3]

The easy way out must be converted into the hard way
upward. *Discipline* is the word. The muscles of morality,
grown flabby with disuse, are now to be made strong by
exercise. The determination to get well is voiced in a
strong command to doctors and nurses and family: "Do
everything you can!" To this is added your promise to
cooperate in every way. Courageous commitment takes
the place of childish comfort as you take the bitter
medicine and undergo the painful exercises.

No pain, no palm;
No thorns, no throne;
No gall, no glory;
No cross, no crown. [4]

Remember the story of the healing of the ten lepers?
"They . . . said, 'Jesus, Master, have pity on us.' Jesus
saw them and said to them, 'Go and let the priests
examine you.' On the way they were made clean" (Luke
17:12-14).

Decision needs the strong incentive of *dedication*. The
answer to "Why do I want to get well?" must be a
positive one. As the Spanish philosopher Ortega y Gasset
once wrote, "Life must be dedicated to a destiny in order
to have meaning." Since there is no place for any hard
bargaining with God, nor any thought that the gift of
healing can be either earned or deserved, the very idea of
getting well must include a purpose in line with that
which you prayerfully believe God wants you to do. This

[3] Robert Browning, *The Ring and the Book,* Book VII, ll. 350-352.
[4] William Penn, *No Cross, No Crown* (London, 1669).

offering of yourself is as gladly and freely made as the blessing is gladly and freely given. Drive and purpose will strengthen your efforts. Respect and cooperation will be inspired in those about you. She had lost her beloved husband within a year. Her hands were terribly gnarled by arthritis. At each weekly service, as she placed her hands in mine for the prayer of healing, she always said: "Please ask God to heal my hands so that I can type again. I want so much to share the great peace I have found with all who have written letters of sympathy." Imagine my joy upon receiving the first letter she had typewritten. And at 82!

Self-diagnosis is not enough. We need someone with divine intuition who sees us as we are and as we can be. And the incredible insight includes a compassion that calls forth a responding obedience. "Get up," said Jesus, "pick up your mat and walk!" (John 5:8). And the man did as he was commanded — and he walked! The late Edwin Arlington Robinson, the mystical poet of Maine, expressed, with true meaning, the power of the impact of Jesus upon the lives of men: "There came along a man who looked at him with such unexpected friendliness and talked with him in such a common way, that life grew marvelously different."

Confession. Forgiveness. Discipline. Dedication. These are the steps we may take to lead us out of the imprisonment of willful sickness into the freedom of zestful living. Spiritual healing is a regeneration of new life in our whole being. This is God's will for all His children, and the way is open to those who will let the divine light and love flow in with power.

9.

How to Pray
for Healing

In the Royal Gallery of Painting at Naples there is a picture portraying how God's help was sought in the midst of a plague that devastated the city in 1656. The background shows the stricken city. In the foreground the sorrowful people are pleading desperately for help to the city officials, who are turning to some Carthusian monks; they in turn are praying to the three patron saints pictured in the sky above; the saints are praying to the Virgin Mary, who is passing along their petitions to Christ; and Christ is offering the prayers to God.

Of course we smile at this idea of prayers traveling up a hierarchical chain of command to God — it seems so childish and mechanical to us. Yet there are people today who think God is very far away, and that He must be approached in a certain way through just the right person. When they are confused about the nature of God,

97

we can suggest that they say, believing, Psalm 23 and the Lord's Prayer, or that they read again the New Testament, especially the Gospels, earnestly seeking to know about Jesus Christ in order to learn what God is like. When they are fearful that God will not be near them in the depth of their need, we can assure them of the truth of the prophet's words: "When you pass through the waters I will be with you; and through the rivers, they shall not overwhelm you" (Isa. 43:2); or just tell them that Jesus never refused to heal or help anyone who came to Him. And when they cannot believe that praying is worthwhile because they cannot conceive of God as being aware of their little cry, we can point to the psalmist's promise: "When he calls to me, I will answer him; I will be with him in trouble" (Ps. 91:15); or exclaim our faith with the words that so quickly leap to our lips, "Ask, and you will receive, seek, and you will find; knock, and the door will be opened to you. For everyone who asks will receive, and he who seeks will find, and the door will be opened to him who knocks" (Matt. 7:7-8; cf. Luke 11:9-10).

The old painting portraying the conception as to how prayer works illustrates another hindrance to prayer for healing. It shows a method of getting God's attention and of trying to influence Him. The modern man of our scientific age is imbued with the necessity of law and order in the universe. To him the very thought of a capricious God is anathema. Quickly we can assure him that he can pray, not in spite of, but in perfect accord with his scientific point of view. When we pray, we do not ask or expect God to break His laws but to enforce *all* of them. Prayer is not a force that breaks through the necessary regularity of the universe, but a spiritual power that lets us receive the benefit of the higher laws which are beyond the ones we know. Therefore we pray that we may appreciate and conform to all the laws God has given for the regularity and justice of the universe according to the best of our human knowledge in order that our obedience may make us willing subjects for the working of His transcendent Spirit.

"Prayer is the soul's sincere desire," sang James Montgomery. Words are the familiar pattern of prayer. They are useful in inspiring us to express that for which we ought to be praying; they help to define our highest aspirations. Sometimes they hide in pious phrases the deep desires of the libido or the selfish wants shielded from sight in the subconscious. A prerequisite to prayer — the prayer before we pray — is the honest effort to put down all that is unworthy and to expose to the penetrating, holy light of God what we really want and why we want it. Then we are ready for the relationship in which we will *let* God speak to us. Then the Spirit of God can come and do His holy work in us.

"Oh, if I only had more faith!" Usually this means a craving for more knowledge of the elements of a certain religious belief. Perhaps the definite teachings of childhood have been blurred or lost altogether. Even more commonly, the cry represents the emptiness of mere creedal faith at a time when utter dependence is needed. A faith devoid of trust will not carry the weight of a crisis. As we grow older, we rely more and more upon man-made powers of protection to the point that religion is sometimes considered an unnecessary crutch. In Christian healing, we include every means at our disposal as provided by God through medical science, without forgetting our need of a childlike trust in the Father. Jesus even goes so far as to say that the confidence that the prayer is already being answered is fundamental to our faith: "For this reason I tell you: When you pray and ask for something, believe that you have received it, and everything will be given you" (Mark 11:24). This is the "prayer of faith."

Dr. Alexis Carrel, the world-famous medical Nobel Prize-winner, once wrote: "Generally, the patient who is cured is not praying for himself. But for another."[1] True prayer for healing can never be selfish. One's own need must always be linked with the needs of others, especially with those in a more desperate state than we are. Even Jesus on the Cross thought of others. His first three words were a prayer of forgiveness, "Father, forgive them, for they know not what they do"; then a message of hope for the thief, "Today shalt thou be with me in paradise"; and lastly, a message of concern for His mother, "Behold thy son . . . . behold thy mother." Bishop Everett H. Jones of West Texas has written a little pamphlet on "How to Pray" in which he uses the points of the cross to symbolize different kinds of prayer. Quite significantly, he indicates the crossing — where the horizontal and vertical lines of the cross meet — as the place to remind us of our need to pray for others. "Intercession," he says, "is love on its knees."

In the Emmanuel Healing Mission in Cleveland,[2] we had some 500 Prayer Partners who had promised to pray for the people who came for help during the service of spiritual healing every Sunday afternoon between four

---

[1] *Man, the Unknown* (New York: Harper & Row, 1935), p. 148.
[2] See Appendix.

and five o'clock. I received a letter from one of the Prayer Partners in Buffalo: "This afternoon as I had one of my very painful attacks of colitis, I knelt at the hour to pray for all those in the Sanctuary, and also for those whose names would be read at the altar during the Intercessions. Suddenly I realized that my own distress had been healed."

"When you pray, endeavor to pray more for others than for yourself alone," wrote John of Cronstadt.[3] As we have seen, it is a natural Christian virtue to pray for others, but the "endeavor" needs direction if our prayers are to be effective. Here, then, are several suggestions as to how to pray for others.

1. *Have a right relationship with the person for whom you pray and for all others.* Certainly you cannot attempt to love one person while you have hatred in your heart for another, for love and hatred are mutually exclusive. In the Sermon on the Mount, Jesus made it a point to say that "if you are about to offer your gift to God at the altar and there you remember that your brother has something against you, leave your gift there in front of the altar and go at once to make peace with your brother; then come back and offer your gift to God" (Matt. 5:23-24; to make this passage more pertinent, try reading it again using the word *prayer* in place of *gift*). This process of reconciliation must include the purging of any thought of judgment upon the one we are to pray for. True prayer for another can hardly allow any semblance of the attitude that he is getting his just desserts. Love, with generous understanding and magnanimity, is the only

---

[3] Quoted by Christopher Woodward in his *Healing Words* (London: Max Parrish, 1958), p. 110.

climate in which prayer for others can live and be effective. To quote John of Cronstadt again: "Pray for all as you would pray for yourself, with the same sincerity and fervor; look upon their infirmities and sicknesses as your own; their temptations, misfortunes, and manifold afflictions as your own. Such prayer will be accepted with great favor by the Heavenly Father, that most gracious, common Father of all." [4]

2. *Secure the cooperation of the person to be prayed for.* It is best if he asks for prayers, to ensure his spiritual belief and cooperation. If he "hates" God for what he thinks has been put upon him by a vengeful Creator, or if he disbelieves in prayer, or even doubts its effectiveness, there will be erected a barrier that God himself cannot break through. It is also important to synchronize the prayer-time. Tell him that you are going to pray for him at a certain hour, so that he can be in a cooperative and receptive mood during those few minutes. If the patient is unconscious, arrange for this prayer-time with those who will be in prayer for him at the same time wherever they are at that moment. Surely we know that distance does not matter. In the ministry of Jesus, we are given the example of the healing of the centurion's son. Jesus simply said the word and the boy was healed at that moment even though Jesus did not go to the centurion's house (Matt. 8:5-13; cf. Luke 7:1-10; John 4:46-53).

3. *Insist upon a hopeful attitude.* If the sick person is sure he is going to die, and if this certainty, or wish, is deeply imbedded in his subconscious, the prayers will hardly avail even though seemingly he may want them.

---

[4] *Ibid.*

Or the others participating in the prayers really may be more concerned with plans for his obsequies or the results of his demise than in earnest prayer for his recovery. A deep doubt or contrary desire will negate the intent of prayers. Better not pray at all than not be absolutely honest in our praying. From the prerequisite of honesty, we move on to the conviction that comes from hope. With our faith strengthened and illumined by the example of Jesus, we are convinced that God cares and that God heals. Then, if the patient really wants God's healing and if we deeply desire his recovery, we can reinforce our prayers with expectant hope. And it will help immeasurably if we visualize the person as getting well or as completely recovered, while we pray to that end.

4. *Always pray for God's blessing as God may see the person's need.* We are tempted to "play God" — to pray as if we knew what was best. We want the sick person to be relieved of his distress and to be restored to the fullness of health. Our faith is shaken if we do not have our prayers answered according to our desires and at the time we think the recovery should come. If we keep in mind that spiritual healing is the healing of the spirit, we allow the possibility that the divine insight may sense the greater importance of spiritual wholeness over physical recovery. Sometimes it may be necessary for a change to take place in the inner self in order to make possible a change in the bodily condition. After all, the soul is more important than the body. In some cases and in God's sight, it may be necessary for the person to experience the physical process of that which we call death in order to achieve that quality of soul required for the person's ongoing development in the new life. We must never lose

sight of our conviction that God has a plan and a purpose for every person, and that in His eternal goal for each individual, life here and hereafter is all of one piece.

5. *Pray — even when your prayers are resisted.* It is not unusual to find a person who definitely resents being prayed for. This resistance may come from his desire to continue willfully his way of life without interference on the part of others — or even God. Fear may play a part in this attitude because he does not want God to get too near. The stubborn insistence upon his freedom to act or live as he wants, come what may, is likely a reaction to a known or unrealized frustration complex. Or there may be deep and hidden factors beyond our poor human ability to fathom. Our natural inclination is to "preach" and scold and nag, which, of course, only increases the resistance to our efforts, no matter how good our intentions may be. Finally we put our judgment upon him and leave him to his "just desserts." But stop! Don't you realize that his bold, outward defiance is primarily a symptom of a deep, inner, and even unrecognized craving for understanding, sympathy, and love? Can it be that the lack of love has made him so unlovable? "Love never fails." And pray for him! His resistance to prayer indicates his need of prayer even more than if he asked for prayer. How pray for him? When he is asleep, his conscious guard is down and the Holy Spirit can touch his subconscious behind the façade of his outward resistance. Set a time for prayer for him regularly each night at an hour when you can assume that he is asleep, and ask other people close to him or interested in him to join in the prayer-tryst for him. Of course, he is not to be told of this. And remember that in such a discipline, no

matter how inconvenient or for how long a time, your sincere efforts, freighted with love and full of faith, will never, never be in vain.

6. *How shall we pray?* We do not have to inform or beseech or cajole God. He is as near as the need. He is as eager to help as we are to pray. Neither do we instruct the Almighty what to do. In the Gospels we note that they simply brought their sick to Jesus in the full confidence that in His presence there was healing. Likewise, we also present our sick to the loving Father with such a self-giving spirit as will enable our spiritual strength to be used in the holy work that needs to be done. Prayer is the catalyst that unlocks and releases God's ready power.

7. *Prayer is belief and trust.* Belief without trust is powerless. Trust without belief is meaningless. God wants us to be well. Perfect wholeness of body, mind, and spirit is His purpose for all His children. Prayer creates a relationship in which His purpose can be accomplished — an opening of the gate to permit His love and healing to flow through to the point of need! Our prayers for others are more than casual wishing or haphazard hoping. The outpouring of our love forms a stream of concern to carry the divine compassion. Therefore, we pray for others in utter confidence because we are in cooperation with a God who cares and who is eager to pour forth His healing power, through any available channel, unto those who need His blessing.

"I prayed for him so earnestly until he died," is an expression frequently heard. The response is: "But why did you stop praying for him?" If we believe that the soul goes on growing after the physical incident of death and if we conceive of the person as entering the new life in the same spiritual state as at the moment of death, then most certainly he needs the continuing benefit of our prayers. Death does not break the bonds of love. As here upon earth, the developing personality continues to depend in a large part upon fellowship with others and a communion of spirit. Every vital religion includes some form of relationship with those who have passed into another existence. In our Christian faith, the Gospel of the Resurrection reveals the quality of life that requires, as well as proclaims, the ongoing of the soul in which we may climb the altar-stairs of development until we approximate the perfection exampled in Jesus Christ.

"Please say a little prayer for me!" This half-jesting, over-the-shoulder parting word always irks me. One day I tried to analyze what the person really meant. Did he think I was able to pray only little prayers? Did it indicate that he could not say even a little prayer by himself for himself? Perhaps we may assume that the matter was a small one needing only a "little prayer" and that he was taking care of the big things himself in some other way. If he thought God was only a little interested, then a "little prayer" would fit exactly the size of the divine concern. If he expected that God could not or would not do very much about the matter anyway, then a "little prayer" would suffice while a "big" prayer would be wasted. To give the petitioner more generous consideration, we might believe that he was trying to build up his faith by testing God to see if He would answer a "little prayer" before venturing to pray a "big prayer" — and that I was invited to share in the experiment. The more I thought about it, the more difficult it became to ascertain the difference between a "little prayer" and a "big prayer." I concluded, finally, that anything worth praying for at all deserved our utmost in prayer because what was important to us was important to God even though the answer might not be in conformity with our expectations. And I thought ,of how prayer is not a matter of a few words, or of many words, or even of a longer or a shorter period of time, but consists of the establishing of a relationship in which perfect trust is primary. Therefore, I solemnly resolved that the next time anyone said, "Please say a little prayer for me," I would give George Macdonald's answer: "I will not say that I will pray for you, but I will think of God and you together."

It is an irresistible temptation to relate the story that the late Rev. Dr. Elwood Worcester told about himself. Once he suffered a severe attack of pneumonia. "For several weeks I had been delirious and quite unconscious of my surroundings. One day my cousin, Dr. Alfred Worcester, managed to attract my attention. He said, 'Elwood, do you know that there is a group of your friends at the church who are praying for you all day long? Don't you think that you ought to pray for yourself?' I agreed to this and called on all the members of my family, the physicians and nurses to kneel around my bed while I prayed, and then immediately I drifted into delirium again. My wife told me it was the greatest prayer she had ever heard. It went on and on until the whole company was weary, and they feared I might die of exhaustion. They kept crying out, 'Amen, Amen. Don't think to be heard for much speaking.' But if any one tried to move, I would rebuke him sternly. So I continued until I could pray no more and I sank into a deep natural sleep. When I awoke, my mind was quite clear and so it remained. That prayer marked the turning point of the illness and from that day, I began to recover."[5]

The above method is hardly to be recommended in spite of its successful outcome. Exclamatory prayers uttered in a state of hysteria or panic are not to be considered conducive to either spiritual or physical therapy. Long experience in praying helps the person to remember the nature of prayer. I recall someone saying that "prayer is the time-exposure of the soul to God." In utter quietness within, we simply place ourselves in the hands of the loving Father. It is not necessary to inform or instruct God. The late John Gaynor Banks was wont to say so often, "Prayer doesn't change God, it changes you." Very often the most helpful kind of prayer is induced by some great affirmations of faith, such as these, for instance, given by Walter DeVoe:

Living Father!
I recognize that my life is one with Thy unlimited life and power.
Thy constructive mind is within me, building my mind and body in strength and perfection.
I open my mind to the influx of Thy mighty presence of health and peace.

"Isn't it selfish to pray for myself?" This question is asked more frequently than one might suppose. Many sincere people are troubled by it. Remember the second great commandment pronounced by Jesus: "You must love your neighbor as yourself" (Matt. 22:39b; cf. Mark 12:31; Luke 10:27). The consideration for others certain-

---

[5] *Making Life Better* (New York: Charles Scribner's Sons, 1932), p. 330.

ly does not negate or lessen the consideration for oneself. The two are inseparably bound together in the worth of each individual, and the holy motive of altruism. We believe that God wants us to be whole in body, mind, and spirit in order that we may fully express our personalities as efficient servants of His in the lifelong ministry of love to others. Then every trace of selfishness is consumed by the warmth of our sacramental self-giving. Love is the keynote and the perpetual theme. Ednah Cheney expresses this thought beautifully in her "Larger Prayer":[6]

> At first I prayed for Light:
>   Could I but see the way,
> How gladly, swiftly would I walk
>   To everlasting day.
>
> And next I prayed for Strength:
>   That I might tread the road
> With firm, unfaltering feet and win
>   The heaven's serene abode.
>
> And then I asked for Faith,
>   Could I but trust my God,
> I'd live enfolded in His peace
>   Though foes were all abroad.
>
> But now I pray for Love:
>   Deep love to God and man,
> A living love that will not fail,
>   However dark His plan.
>
> And Light and Strength and Faith,
>   Are opening everywhere:
> God waited for me till
>   I prayed the larger prayer.

[6] Ednah D. Cheney, *Reminiscences of Ednah D. Cheney* (New York: Lothrop, Lee and Shepard, 1902), pp. 175-176.

In writing on prayer, Elwood Worcester made a point of "The Law of Sincerity: The essence of prayer lies in direct, vital commerce with God as a Friend. All genuine human friendship is based on reality and veracity on both sides."[7] In other words, complete and utter honesty with God and ourselves is a positive prerequisite of prayer. Nothing can be hidden. An inner sense of guilt, either real or imagined, can form an opaque barrier through which the healing light cannot pass. It is not possible to pray for healing when we are nagged by the idea, even though untrue, that God has sent the sickness as punishment, or when we think we are unworthy to receive the blessing we so much need. Sometimes we have to face the plain fact that our distress is really the result of a foolish act or careless neglect or even anxiety getting out of hand. Dare we suggest that a prayer for forgiveness might well precede the prayer for healing?

"I want to be well!" is the burden of our cry. Why? What we want is not half as important as *why* we want it. Is it just to be relieved of pain or to be freed from a physical handicap or to be able to live as we lived before and be the same as we always were? The crisis of illness is a time to examine our wishes and clarify our motives. On a few occasions I have dared to ask a person: "Why do you want to be healed?" In most cases, the confusion has been as pitiful as the resentment. God knows us, and He has the right to expect a spirit worthy of the blessing for which we ask. Deep in our hearts there is a craving to be better and to be able to express ourselves to the fullest in the service of others. In the laying-on of hands,[8] I prefer

---

[7] Elwood Worcester and Samuel McComb, *Body, Mind and Spirit* (Boston: Marshall Jones, 1931), p. 330.

[8] See Appendix.

to meet each person alone at the kneeling place so that, in privacy, I can learn the person's first name and ask: "What shall we pray for?" It has been an amazing experience to have so many make spiritual requests — even though their illnesses or handicaps were very obvious — to be helpful to others, to be more patient with husband or wife, to develop Christian virtues. Spiritual healing is first of all the healing of the spirit.

Another prerequisite of the prayer for the healing of oneself is the conviction that God does care for you. One good exercise toward this assurance is to recount the goodness of God toward you through the past years. Remember the line of the old evangelistic song: "Count your many blessings; name them one by one"? And try reading through the Gospels to note that Jesus never failed to heal a single person who came to Him or was brought to Him. Our entire Christian faith is predicated upon the importance of every individual. Without this fundamental belief, prayer becomes a meaningless gesture. But when you are sure that God cares, your approach carries the confidence of a hurt child running into the arms of a loving father. Dr. Alexis Carrel tells this story of great insight: "An old peasant was seated alone in the last pew of the village church. 'What are you waiting for?' he was asked; he answered, 'I am looking at Him and He is looking at me.'" [9]

A discussion of how to pray for healing would hardly be complete without considering the oft-quoted petition of the Lord's Prayer: "May your will be done on earth as it is in heaven" (Matt. 6:10b). Unfortunately, it is used mostly in a negative way which stultifies the hopeful

---

[9] *Prayer Is Power* (Cincinnati: Forward Movement Publications, n.d.).

spirit so necessary to prayer. It carries the assumption that God sends sickness to punish us or to make us better. It limits the power of God to heal us by increasing doubt instead of faith and by causing us to dwell upon our sickness rather than upon God's will that we be well. In fact, if we should carry this idea to its logical conclusion, we would have to consider it a sin against God's will to use any means — even medical — toward our healing, especially prayer. Such a supine resignation in the name of religion is false piety. It is a denial of everything we know about life and God. Emily Gardiner Neal puts it emphatically: "'Thy Will Be Done' has long been prayed as a lugubrious accompaniment to hopeless situations, and the phrase seems to have become a natural corollary to disaster." [10]

But there is another side to the coin. This is found by using the whole of the petition: "May your will be done on earth as it is in heaven" (Matt. 6:10b). Instead of something to be borne, the will of God is something to be done in harmony with the Kingdom which is and is to come. The emphasis is constructive and positive. It has to do with moral values. It reveals the way of wholesomeness that makes for wholeness. It is the antidote for sin and sickness. "Nearly all human pain, suffering and disease," declares Weatherhead, "come from human folly, ignorance and sin. The will of God is that man should replace folly with wisdom, ignorance with knowledge, and sin with holiness. Nothing, therefore, that is the fruit of folly, ignorance and sin can possibly be the will of God in the sense of being His intention." [11]

[10] God Can Heal You Now (Englewood Cliffs, N.J.: Prentice-Hall, 1958), p. 17.

[11] Psychology, Religion and Healing (Rev. ed.; Nashville: Abingdon Press, 1952), p. 187.

In conclusion and to summarize, it may be helpful to present as a sort of rule of thumb the following guidelines, as we pray for healing:

Be reconciled. Get right with God and with anyone against whom you have any grievance or resentment whatsoever. Both forgive and be forgiven.

Relinquish. Sincerely put your need in the hands of God, and leave it there. Go on about the business of doing everything possible, to the limit of your power, and entrust the humanly impossible to God's power.

Relax. Tension, especially that caused by fear, is a certain barrier to the inflowing of the healing power. Pray in a state of complete ease of mind with every muscle relaxed, and with the spirit at rest in the love of the Heavenly Father. "Let go and let God!"

Believe. This goes beyond academic faith and creedal form. It assumes a knowledge of Christian truth and a tireless reading of the Bible. We mean belief in God that has matured into trust of God.

Dedicate. Devote the faculties you have to God's service so that both He and you will know that when the blessing comes, all of your abilities will be used in His Name and to His glory.

A Prayer in Time of Illness

O God my Father, who in love has created me Thy child, grant me to be sure that Thou dost know my need as I look to Thee for help. Accept my thanks for all Thy blessings, Thy gift of good health in years past, and for all Thou art doing for me even now. Let not my pain make me forget others who also are suffering, and for whom I would pray even before myself, especially for those whose burden is greater than my own.

Cast out of my body, mind, and spirit any evil

thing Thou mayest find within me, cleanse me from all sin, and create in me the will to live by Thy laws. Hear me as I promise to give unto Thee in good works my whole self and my every talent. When I have to suffer, may I do so in patience, in constant thanks for the care I receive, and in such nobleness that others may gain courage from my example. Though this hour may be dark, inspire me to think only of good things and good health.

Now may Thy hand of healing be upon me. Cool my fevered brow. Calm my restless spirit. Comfort me as a mother stills her child. And send forth Thy new life within me until I shall be whole again. May Thy will be done unto me according to Thy purpose and in the measure of my need. So hear me, O God, as I pray in the name of Thy Son, Jesus Christ — my Lord, my Saviour, and my Friend, in heaven and on earth. Amen. [12]

---

[12] By Laurence H. Blackburn.

10.

The Redemptive
Quality of
Spiritual Healing

"Jesus as the Messiah was the bringer of 'health and salvation.' Jesus as the Savior ministered both in the religious sense of salvation and in the sense of healing a disease. One cannot separate Jesus' healing ministry from His redemptive mission. Each is inextricably woven into one whole."[1]

Emily Gardiner Neal's first book, *A Reporter Finds God through Spiritual Healing*,[2] is still my primary recommendation to those who desire an introduction to the subject. In relating her experiences in writing it, she told me one day that she undertook to visit every one of the cases referred to her, for she wanted to see the people

---

[1] From the Introduction to the *Report of the Joint Commission on the Ministry of Healing*, adopted unanimously by the General Convention of the Episcopal Church, 1964.

[2] (New York: Morehouse-Barlow Co., 1956).

about whose healing she was writing. Her husband,
Alvin, to whom she dedicates the book, accompanied her
on many of these calls to the homes. One evening as they
concluded their work, he remarked quite casually, "You
know, I can always tell the member of the family who has
been healed even before he is pointed out. There's a sort
of translucent light about his face, his eyes are brighter,
he looks alive — he's different!"

Jesus came revealing the prophesied Messiah as the
Son of God and the Son of man. Jesus came transcending
the idea of a political kingdom with the ideal of a
spiritual Rule of God in the hearts of men. Jesus came
regenerating the conception of God from that of a
judging King to a loving Father. Jesus came uplifting
men from being slaves to the senses to becoming con-
querors over every condition of life. And Jesus came
healing! Is it not reasonable to believe that He saw in the
use of the healing power a redemptive quality? That each
person He touched with His blessing not only might be
spared from suffering but saved for spiritual living on a
higher plane? Multitudes were healed by Jesus. Most of
the individual healings lack satisfactory description. Yet
it is logical to assume that many believers in the early
days came from among those whose lives had been
touched by one Jesus of Nazareth, now proclaimed the
Christ of God. Human gratitude would demand nothing
less. It is inconceivable to think that the Master's
blessing of sight to a blind man did not eventually help
him to see life differently. One miracle illustrates this
change in personality in dramatic fashion. It is the story
of the madman among the tombs in the land of the
Gerasenes across the lake of Galilee (Matt. 8:28-34; cf.

Mark 5:1-20; Luke 8:26-39). He is described as being too strong to be held by the chains put upon him, as crying out day and night in the desolate place, as naked, and as cutting himself with sharp stones. Jesus cast out the demons that were tormenting him. Word of this spread quickly. From the nearby city, "people went out to see what had happened. They came to Jesus and found the man from whom the demons had gone out, sitting at the feet of Jesus, clothed, and in his right mind" (Luke 8:35).

In that land and in that time, it was common to call sin the source of sickness. Jesus did not accept entirely this universal idea, as His diverse methods in healing plainly show. Yet there are some instances which reveal that His divine intuition clearly detected sin as the cause of the ailment. In the dramatic healing of the man at the Pool of Bethesda (John 5: 1-16, especially v. 14b) there is no mention of the nature of his illness or of its cause; but when Jesus met him in the Temple, there was this significant warning: "Look, you are well now. Quit your sins, for something worse may happen to you." This represents a positive illustration of the redemptive quality in the miracle; and we may assume that many more of Jesus' healing miracles would reveal this same quality if all the facts had been recorded in the Gospels. Alan Richardson claims that "the connection between healing and salvation (in the religious sense) is a characteristic feature of the Gospel tradition. Miracles of healing were, as it were, symbolic demonstrations of God's forgiveness in action."[3]

---

[3] *The Miracle Stories of the Gospels* (London: SCM Press, 1956), pp. 61-62.

Even more dramatic is the miracle at Capernaum (Matt. 9: 1-8, especially v. 2; cf. Mark 2: 1-12 and Luke 5: 17-26) where there was such a crush of people in the house to hear Jesus that some friends or possibly relatives of a paralyzed young man had to let him down through a hole in the roof to get him to the feet of the Master. Without hesitation, Jesus, seeing their faith, said to the sick man: "My son, your sins are forgiven." This prompted the argumentative listeners to challenge Jesus' authority to forgive sins. Jesus' response was that in this case, the pronouncement of forgiveness was equivalent to the command to rise up and walk.

Modern psychotherapy verifies this. When I conducted a spiritual healing pilgrimage to Europe in 1960, we went to Geneva for the purpose of seeing my friend, the Rev. Bernard Martin, who as a pastor had long been interested in the modern healing ministry and had written several popular books on the subject. [4] At the time of our visit he was chaplain of the state mental hospital in his city, and he related to us the progress being made at the hospital by a team-ministry program. It was an unforgettable experience to hear him tell of the case of a young man who was completely paralyzed and unable to talk. Thorough examination by the physicians proved that there was no organic reason why he could not move. The psychiatrists concluded that the cause of his paralysis was fear. Careful interrogation of relatives coupled with pastoral experience and not a little intuition led the chaplain to believe that back of the fear was a guilt

---

[4] Since then, *The Healing Ministry in the Church* (1960) and *Healing for You* (1967), both published by the John Knox Press of Richmond.

complex. Day after day, the chaplain talked quietly with the patient about God's love and forgiveness. Always there was the reading of carefully selected verses from the Bible, and a prayer that related the deepseated need to the grace of Jesus Christ. The ministrations of the physicians and the psychiatrists continued too, while the chaplain slowly gained the patient's confidence until there was noticeable response. Then came the appointed day. While the doctors stood in the background, Chaplain Martin talked with the patient in a low, earnest voice, concluding with such words as these: "Now, my boy, everything is all right. God has completely forgiven you. You don't need to be afraid any more." Then in a loud commanding voice: "Get up, son, and walk! You are healed! You are well! You are free!" And the young man got up — and walked! From being frozen by fear through morbid guilt, he was restored to wholeness of body, mind, and spirit through forgiveness. Dr. Weatherhead thinks very strongly about this: "The forgiveness of God, in my opinion, is the most powerful therapeutic idea in the world. If a person really believes that God has forgiven him, then the burden of guilt and the fear at the heart of it disappear."[5] And later, he testifies that "I have never, in thirty years, known a psychological treatment which, in this field of guilt, could by itself obtain freedom for the patient without recourse to all that the Christian religion offers."[6]

If "sick emotions breed sick bodies," then healing to the point of wholeness must include a therapy deep

---

[5] *Psychology, Religion and Healing* (Rev. ed.; Nashville: Abingdon Press, 1952), p. 334.
[6] *Ibid.,* p. 342.

enough to touch and change the fundamental causes. Physicians are well aware of the need for this psychophysiological approach, but are not equipped by training, nor do they have the time, to get at the deep-seated causes and prescribe the necessary treatment. In dealing with the sick mind, the psychiatrists find it necessary not only to discover the underlying causes of the aberrations but also to work toward the establishing of a new pattern of thinking. Dr. Arthur P. Noyes, M.D., relates his effort in these words: "To quite an extent the therapist becomes an educator and explainer of the patients' life experiences and reactions. Among his objectives is that of re-educating conscious attitudes which have been warped by resentment, guilt, hostility, frustration, overambition or depression.... It is hoped there may be a certain reintegration of the personality with increased harmony and internal balance."[7] And Dr. Noyes also describes the therapy of psychoanalysis in similar terms: "The analyst seeks to bring about changes in personality structure by undoing the unfavorable patterns established in earlier years. Psychoanalysis aims to explore the deeper layers of the patient's mind with the hope that thereby, he may acquire a maximum of self-knowledge and effect an alteration in the structure of his personality by undoing and reorganizing the unfavorable patterns that were established in an earlier period."[8]

Some psychiatrists have found that their analyses and their therapies are definitely related to religion. One is here reminded of C. G. Jung's famous declaration:

---

[7] Arthur P. Noyes and Laurence C. Kolb, *Modern Clinical Psychiatry* (5th ed.; Philadelphia, W. B. Saunders Co., 1958), p. 626.
[8] *Ibid.*, p. 627.

"During the past thirty years, people from all the civilized countries of the earth have consulted me.... Among my patients in the second half of life — that is to say over thirty-five, there has not been one whose problem in the last resort was not that of finding a religious outlook on life. It is safe to say that every one of them fell ill because he had lost that which the living religions of every age had given to their followers and none of them has been really healed who did not regain this religious outlook."[9]

We define spiritual healing as the healing of the spirit. Therefore, it is more than relief from pain, freedom from a handicap, or even mental adjustment. It deals with the causative sickness within the soul of man — the seat of his emotions and the center of his personality structure. Its goal is wholeness, with the body, mind, and spirit thoroughly integrated and perfectly balanced. To accomplish this, its therapeutics must be essentially spiritual. In sickness, a search is made to discover the psychosomatic cause in order that the healing may reach to the depth of the real need. If there is no trace of inner disease or tension, a spiritual approach nevertheless is necessary in order to avoid the idea of fatalism — "this is just my fate"; or a martyrdom complex — "this is something I've just got to endure." To blame God destroys the necessary relationship with God. To continue a desperate stoicism causes inner tension which may counteract the therapeutic process. If the healing is delayed or incomplete, it is important that the ministry of healing shall have been, and continue to be, on a spiritual basis so as to enable the

---

[9] *Modern Man in Search of a Soul* (New York: Harcourt, Brace and World, 1933), p. 229.

person to live above his pain without self-pity in the triumph of a mature soul. If healing does come, it is still necessary that it include a redemptive quality sufficient to eliminate the underlying emotional causes and to prevent the person from falling again into the pattern of life that led down the path to the sickness. Hear the testimony of Dr. Albert Reissner, a Brooklyn psychoanalyst: "More and more of us are becoming convinced of two things: first, that man is a trinity composed of body, mind, and spirit: and second, that the underlying cause of most disease is spiritual. We have observed that unless a healing of the spirit takes place, the cure of the body or mind is not apt to be either complete or permanent."

Several years ago, I was invited to conduct a spiritual healing mission in a midwestern city. It was held in a large church which had forty doctors as members, and a dinner meeting was arranged for them. Afterward one of the doctors drew me into a quiet corner and told me this unforgettable story of his own experience. Early in life, he had developed into a perfectionist. In striving for the ideal he had become acutely conscious of anything less than the perfect. This led him to become resentful of others who were not like-minded. Born into a strongly Protestant tradition, through several unfortunate experiences his perfectionism yielded to prejudice, especially against Roman Catholics. Then he began to suffer from a severe pain his back. It came and went spasmodically. At times it was so severe as to handicap him seriously in his professional duties. Various specialists to whom he went could find no physical basis for his pain; and even the Mayo Clinic sent him home to live with his backache and to take medicine to alleviate the pain. One day, while attending a medical convention in New York, he found himself walking down Fifth Avenue during the lunch hour, and was caught up in the crowd entering St. Patrick's Cathedral. There he saw the people worshiping in a way he could neither believe in nor understand. His old prejudices welled up to the point of resentment, as he walked down the side aisle. Suddenly came the pain in his back. It was almost unbearable. It bent him over. At the chancel steps, he had to pause to catch his breath, and he wondered if he would ever be able to get to the door. Somehow, he was impelled to look up, in spite of the added pain it caused. Almost directly above him was a life-size crucifix. He had not seen it there when he entered the Cathedral. Was it a vision? Had it been let down from somewhere just for him? But it was certainly real, for he reached up and touched the wood of the cross. He saw the hands of the Christ outstretched on the cross. Then, for the first time in his life, his eyes beheld the Christ welcoming all who would come to Him, whatever their mode of worship. He stood there at the foot of the cross for a long time, until his sense of propriety made him feel that he might be uncomfortably conspicuous in such a prominent place. As he hurried down the other side aisle toward the door, he became aware that he was walking upright. At the door, he paused to look back. The cross was gone — and so was his pain! And how well I remember his concluding words: "I can tell you honestly that from that moment, there has never been a trace of the old pain. Something really happened to me that day as I stood at the foot of the Cross!"

Explain it? The doctor did not even attempt an

explanation. Perhaps a psychiatrist could indicate the inner processes at work. We know that resentment causes tension and that tension causes pain. But we also know that when anyone in dire need of healing comes to the foot of the Cross and, in his agony, looks up to behold the agony on the face of the Man with arms outstretched upon the wood, something happens — and it is both redemptive and healing. Pastor Bernard Martin quotes Matthew 8:17, "where healing by the power of the Lord is put under the very sign of the Cross: 'That it might be fulfilled which was spoken by Isaias the prophet, saying Himself took our infirmities, and bare our sicknesses.' Here we have an absolutely clear indication of the link between the work of spiritual redemption and that of healing. Fundamentally, there is no real distinction between the two. Jesus wills the salvation of men. In giving them, through expiation, release from the power of sin, He has included release from that external and visible sign of sin which is disease."[10]

---

[10] *The Healing Ministry in the Church* (Richmond: John Knox Press, 1960), p. 56.

11.

When Healing Doesn't Seem to Come

"There are no failures in spiritual healing," writes Emily Gardiner Neal at the end of her first book.[1] We are startled by such a bold statement even though we recognize the thorough research that preceded it and are aware of the overwhelming conviction that prompted it.

"No failures!" "Preposterous." "I don't believe it." "How many times I've prayed for healing and nothing happened." "Take the case of Uncle Charlie." "I've been to healing services where no one seemed to get any help at all." "Does she mean that every prayer is answered?"

The chorus of objection is loud and vehement. But in all fairness we should read further to note the author's

---

[1] *A Reporter Finds God Through Spiritual Healing* (New York: Morehouse-Barlow Co., 1956).

words to support her controversial claim: "No one who
has felt the healing power, whether or not he has been
physically healed, remains spiritually unchanged. He is
the recipient of unseen but none the less positive stig-
mata, the marks of which he will carry always on his
soul. He has received an inpouring of spiritual grace
which, in turning him to the Lord in faith, gratitude and
service, has transformed his life."

Brave words written out of great conviction! Will they
prove to be true for us when we have tried to resolve some
of the problems that confront us when healing doesn't
seem to come?

One of these problems is the blunt and obvious fact
that some are healed and others are not. No doctor would
ever claim that he never lost a patient. No healer would
ever claim that everyone receiving his ministrations is
healed, even though he may talk about his successes and
try to forget his failures. No one who has prayed
earnestly for the healing of others would ever claim that
all his prayers were answered in the way he wished.

A case in point is Lourdes. It is estimated that two
million visitors and thirty thousand sick people go to this
famous shrine in the south of France every year. Count-
less thousands drink the water from the sacred spring and
some 2,500 are given the baths every day. Yet so careful
is the investigation that only 51 miraculous cures have
been declared by the Roman Catholic Church in nearly
one hundred years. In 1953, the president of the Medical
Bureau stated: "We have some 1200 records and files of
'inexplicable' cures for which we have systematic and
orderly accounts. ... We have notations and material
concerning some 4,000 cases that are very probably

complete and genuine cures." And Ruth Cranston adds that "it is probably safe to say that at least ten thousand people have been cured there."[2] Even considering those who receive complete or partial healing at home afterward and do not bother to undergo the exhaustive examinations necessary to file a report with the Bureau at Lourdes, the number of cures is a minute fraction of the sick persons who have sought a miracle there during these hundred years. Yet who would dare to disparage Lourdes because only a comparative few receive healing? Shall we wait to evaluate the shrine until there is an answer to the imponderable question as to why some are healed and others are not?

There were some doubts in my mind about its being worthwhile to make the long trip to Lourdes from Paris. Fortunately, I shared my questioning with our waiter at the hotel and found that he had come from Lourdes. "Go, by all means," he said. "It is a place of spiritual pilgrimage."

"Will I see any miracles"? I asked naïvely.

"Probably not," he replied, "but you will be inspired by the great faith of the people there."

It was an indescribable experience. Twenty to thirty thousand visitors were there and most of them marched in the long procession which reached its climax in the great square in front of the basilica where the hundreds of hand-drawn carriages and stretchers bore the sick ones hopefully awaiting the blessing. Of course there had been the mingling with the silent throngs at the grotto and the observing of the scores of *brancardiers* tenderly carrying

[2] *The Miracle of Lourdes* (New York: McGraw-Hill Book Co., 1955), p. 136.

the sick into the baths. These men volunteer their services out of gratitude for blessings that have come either to them or to a relative or friend. Then came the magnificent candlelight procession with the continuous "Ave, Maria," so overwhelming and uplifting that one was sure it was reaching the Throne of Heaven above the blue, starlit sky. And when I took the Spiritual Healing Pilgrimage Party there three years later, the experience was even more moving. No, I didn't see any miracles, and frankly, I wondered about those hundreds of sick people going home in bitter disappointment and broken faith. No so, says Ruth Cranston: "Even when no physical cure takes place, it has been noted time and again that the most important thing that happens at Lourdes is the cure of souls. Those who have to go back, and live on with their physical miseries, seem to get such a spiritual transformation and inspiration that they can go on cheerfully and gratefully." [3]

Another problem is that of partial healing. We are concerned about the person who goes out from a service of Spiritual Healing saying, "Yes, I think I feel a little better." While we are glad for any betterment that comes, we pray always for complete healing. Our faith and our expectation must not limit the power of a God who wants us to be well.

Among all the healing miracles of our Lord, only one provides an example of partial healing. It happened at Bethsaida, where a blind man was brought to Jesus, who touched his eyes and asked him, "Can you see anything?" The man looked up and said: "I can see men, but they

---

[3] *Ibid.*, p. 139.

look like trees walking around." Jesus again placed his hands on the man's eyes. This time the man looked hard, his eyesight came back, and he saw everything clearly (Mark 8:23c-25). Was the man lacking in faith or expectation? We can only surmise the reason for the partial healing when Jesus first touched him. One clue is given, however. It may have been the doubts of those with whom he was associated where he lived, for "Jesus then sent him home with the order, 'Don't go back into the village'" (Mark 8:26).

Later we will discuss more fully what to do when healing doesn't seem to come, but here it should be said, in answer to the question asked many times, that a person is invited and urged to come to the services of spiritual healing regularly — to give thanks to God for the blessings received, to keep the benefits bestowed through continued spiritual uplift, and to seek the complete healing we are sure God wants for us.

Closely related to partial healing is delayed healing. Our impatient natures demand immediate action even though we do not expect it from medicine and we are willing to undergo long series of treatments if necessary. The healing miracles of Jesus have contributed to our thinking that all healing of God must be instantaneous, for all of them — with the possible exception of the incident of the ten lepers (Luke 17:11-19) — describe an immediate result. It is a common experience to attend many services of spiritual healing or even Healing Missions without experiencing any noticeable benefit oneself or witnessing any change in others. "Nothing seemed to happen at all," is the disappointing dictum. While dramatic healings do occur, it is more usual to find the blessing taking effect afterward. A letter picked at random from my files contains this oft-repeated statement: "Following that service, the constant pain left." When we consider the tangle our nature can get into to cause our sickness, according to the psychosomatic approach, and when we realize how long these degenerative factors have been at work, as well as our congenital resistance to change even from worse to better, we recognize how extraordinarily powerful are the forces that combine to produce an instantaneous healing miracle. A delayed healing may not mean that nothing is happening, but that the physical aspects of the healing process are not as yet visible or felt. After all, delayed healing is still healing, no matter how long it may take, even though it is a severe test of our faith when healing doesn't seem to come at once.

Our first reaction in our disappointment is to blame someone. It is easy to point to God as the cause of the failure. When we see others healed and we are not, we fall into the trap of thinking of God as being capricious and playing favorites, or that He is limited in His power to heal certain diseases. But Pastor Martin emphasizes that "in the whole Bible there is no text which can make us think that the divine will to heal may have certain exceptions."[4] Another object of our blame is the so-called healer as we criticize his sincerity or his claim of spiritual power, and include him in our condemnation of the healing ministry or even the Church itself. More generous souls take the blame themselves and become dangerously introspective as they think the failure has

---

[4]Bernard Martin, *The Healing Ministry in the Church* (Richmond: John Knox Press, 1960), p. 107.

come because of their lack of faith or their unworthiness. Again I yield to Pastor Martin's strong words: "A failure can be a sign of our individual and collective unbelief, but never a sign of the limitations of the power or love of God."[5]

What shall we do when healing doesn't seem to come? It is evident that we need a positive and constructive approach to the problem. Here are five steps that will be helpful to follow:

1. *Let go of your doubts.* One of the most insidious elements involved is that of becoming content with pain or a handicap and conditioned to the care that accompanies sickness. This engenders a lamentable hopelessness that sometimes induces morbid introspection within and cruel criticism without. Know that God wants you to be well. Rise up to escape the web of oversolicitation woven about you. Break the chains of doubt with which others hold you down because of their lack of faith. Even Jesus found it impossible to do anything miraculous in His hometown because the doubts of the people made Him powerless to heal except in a small way (Matt 13: 53-58; cf. Mark 6: 1-6). *Want* to be healed. *Expect* that you will be healed. *Pray* with calm assurance and utter faith. *Know* that the Living Presence is as near as your need, with as much power to heal as compassion to feel. *Believe* this. *Let* the power come. And if doubts assail, remember the prayer of the father before Jesus healed his son: "I do have faith, but not enough. Help me!" (Mark 9:24).

2. *Examine your motives.* It may be that you are seeking health for the wrong reasons. Behind our sore

---

[5] *Ibid.*, p. 105.

disappointment, there may lurk these unspoken questions tinged with envy: "Why was he healed when I was not? Am I not just as good? Does it mean that God cares more for him than He does for me?" Perhaps you want physical healing without the willingness to accept its spiritual concomitant. Is there a pet sin standing in the way? To ask God's forgiveness could be your first step, along with a sincere promise to lead a new life and to obey God's physical and moral laws. God's forgiveness of us requires our forgiveness of others, as conversely, our forgiveness of others makes possible God's forgiveness of us. Jesus told the disciples, "And when you stand praying, forgive whatever you have against anyone, so that your Father in heaven will forgive your sins" (Mark 11:25).

A common block to healing is found to be a wrong relationship. A classic illustration is found in the tragic story of Cecil Rhodes, that builder of an empire in South Africa. When his dreams of conquest began to fade, he blamed others and then developed an intense hatred toward every friend he had. In dismay, they saw his tremendous physique succumb to the ravages of disease brought on by the tension of extreme hatred. His physicians did everything possible to save his life, but without avail, because his fundamental sickness was in his heart. "Love is the perfect antidote that floods the mind to wash away hatred, jealousy, resentment, anxiety and fear."[6] Then there is selfishness and self-centeredness, which have to be counteracted by a thoroughgoing dedication to the service of others. Will you answer this question honestly, "Why do I want to be healed?"

---

[6] Wilfred A. Peterson in *This Week* magazine, October 27, 1963.

An English divine has rightly said that "Failure to obtain healing is a stern challenge to submit our whole being to God's scrutiny."[7]

3. *Grow spiritually.* When healing doesn't seem to come, thwart the temptation to turn disappointment into bitterness by a determined effort to grow in the things of the spirit. The discipline of reading inspired literature will provide an uplift. Choose some of the most stimulating passages of the Bible and read them over and over. Here are a few suggestions: Psalms 23, 91, 103, 116; the Sermon on the Mount, Matthew 5, 6, and 7; St. Paul's exposition of the new life in Christ, Romans 8; and his sermon on Christian love, 1 Corinthians 13. Become so familiar with Jesus' healing miracles that you can visualize each one. Learn the supreme truths of Christ's teaching until they become essential to your life and thought. The ten lepers were evidently not cleansed of the disease at once, but Jesus told them what to do. "On the way they were made clean" (Luke 17: 11-19).

A man came to our service of spiritual healing and most earnestly requested the laying-on of hands for a serious heart ailment. Afterward he wrote me a wonderful letter about all that the experience had meant to him, and I am permitted to share this one paragraph with you: "Because the healing was not complete, I began to examine my spiritual life critically. In the light of this self-examination, I discovered that what I had considered to be a good Christian life had many defects. I have been making an effort to rectify these defects, and I think that I am making progress, and with God's help, I will gain complete healing."

[7] E. Howard Cobb, *Christ Healing* (London: Marshall, Morgan & Scott, 1954), p. 106.

4. *Keep on praying.* It is distressing to witness the agony of spirit in those who have experienced a seeming failure of their hopes and expectations for healing through prayer. "God doesn't hear my prayers." "I just can't pray any more." "Don't bother to pray for me. It won't do any good." Having in mind what we have considered in a previous chapter on praying for healing, and in view of the three steps just outlined, our strong advice is to keep on praying. Real prayer is never in vain. Like substance, the spiritual energy created by prayer may be changed in form but never destroyed. The world-famous Dr. Carrel stated that "Prayer is . . . the most powerful form of energy that one can generate. The influence of prayer on the human mind and body is as demonstrable as that of secreting glands. . . . It could not happen that any man or woman could pray for a single moment, without some good result."[8] So let us replace our shortsightedness and impatience with conviction and courage. And persist in prayer! In His parable of the importunate friend (Luke 11:5-8), Jesus pointed out the necessity of perseverance in prayer, and added these irrevocable words, "Ask and you will receive; seek, and you will find; knock, and the door will be opened to you. For everyone who asks will receive, and he who seeks will find, and the door will be opened to him who knocks" (Luke 11:9-10; cf. Matt. 7:7-8). Such assurance is not modified, but only lengthened, by the omission of exactly when or how our prayers will be answered. We believe, but the test of faith is trust.

---

[8] *Prayer Is Power* (Cincinnati: Forward Movement Publications, n.d.).

I know not by what methods rare,
But this I know — God answers prayer . . .
I know not when He sends the word
That tells us fervent prayer is heard.
I know it cometh — soon or late;
Therefore we need to pray and wait.
I know not if the blessing sought
Will come in just the way I thought.
I leave my prayers with Him alone,
Whose Will is wiser than my own. [9]

5. *Overcome the fear of death.* Whether innate or inbred, the fear of death is deeply ingrained in our nature. It is almost universal. It is thought of as the last and inescapable "enemy" of life, and it would seem to thwart the plan of the Almighty. Yet as everyone is born, so everyone dies. God is responsible. He made us this way. It must be for good. Death is as natural as it is inevitable. It is a physical incident in the ongoing life of the person, for we are souls clothed with a body in order to express ourselves while on this physical plane of life. Since God never negates His creation, death must be a release from the burden of the body in order to claim a freer existence in a purely spiritual life. Then that which we call death becomes a step in the growth of the soul and may be, if we will but let it, a welcome stage in the therapy of our whole person. When healing doesn't seem to come, we prevent its possibility by giving up to the insidious fear of death. Of all times, this is when we must lay hold of our faith in the transcendence of life by a triumphant God. At

---

[9] Anonymous. Quoted by Christopher Woodward in *Healing Words* (London: Max Parrish and Co., 1958), p. 83.

a large dinner meeting, a young man rushed up to me, shook my hand warmly, and exclaimed, "Thank you, thank you, thank you for all you did for my wife and for me during her illness." I could only look at him, for, at the moment, I did not recognize him nor remember the incident. I was saved from asking about her for he fairly poured forth the story. "Yes, as you remember, she had cancer and died a few weeks after we came up to your church for counseling and for the laying-on of hands. You will never know how much that meant to her and to me, as we faced together her passing, especially when she was so young. And you may think it very strange, but I feel closer to her in a spiritual way than I ever did while she was with us. Perhaps we've both grown a lot since that day. Thank you!" Of course, I was quite speechless. I had thought there *could* be such an expression of gratitude, but never in such a very real and dramatic way. And when I came across these words of the Rev. Richard Spread of England, I realized their truth as never before: "Spiritual healing is essentially spiritual in character. This accounts for the fact that those who do not receive physical healing do not lose their faith in God. They always receive spiritual grace."

Throughout our discussion about healing that doesn't seem to come, there may have been lurking in your mind the story of St. Paul's "thorn in the flesh" (2 Cor. 12:1-10). The general assumption is that it was a debilitating physical handicap of some kind, although its nature has been debated for centuries. While Paul says that the "thorn" was given by "a messenger of Satan," the context reveals that God allowed it. Paul believed the "thorn in the flesh" had been given to curb his pride, for he had been boasting of the extraordinary experiences in the spirit which had come to him. He was hardly given to humility. This came as a lesson to prove the necessity of this grace if he was to bear the message of his Christ. The punishment accomplished this end, but Paul feared that if it were not taken away, he would be unable to carry out his God-given mission effectively. Therefore, he prayed three times that the "thorn" might be removed. But God saw fit to use him more powerfully with a suffering body than without it. Paul learned that when he was weak, he was strong. The experience threw him back upon a really victorious trust in God's power — that He could do so much with so little! Paul's prayer for relief from the distressing "thorn in the flesh" was not answered as he had prayed, nor at the time when he thought he needed to be relieved of it. God was achieving, through pain, a greater purpose within the soul of His chosen one. It is believed that the condition eventually passed away because Paul wrote to the Galatians (4:13) that he no longer had the infirmity which they had observed on his first visit to them. The entire experience must be viewed in relation to Paul's mission for Christ. He learned by this and other hardships that the Way was not an easy one, and that perfect trust was a necessary attribute if he was to continue to follow when he could not understand. Think of the saints, both ancient and modern, who have made a bed or a wheelchair a throne of grace! When healing did not come to Paul as he prayed, the answer was, "My grace is all you need; my power is strongest when you are weak" (2 Cor. 12:9).

Failure can lead us to a debilitating defeatism or sting us into positive action. At a crucial moment in World

War I, Marshal Foch sent this message: "My left is crushed. My right is in retreat. The situation is excellent. I move to attack."

When healing doesn't seem to come provides just the right time to take stock of our praying, of our methods, and of ourselves. If our objective is only to get well physically, then the seeming failure is deserved. The disappointing experience, if we will but let it, will lead us to a spiritual conception of wholeness. When we come into the presence of the living Christ, we hear Him ask, as He asked the blind beggar on the Jericho road, "What do you want me to do for you?" (Luke 18: 41; cf. Matt. 20: 32; Mark 10: 51) What will our answer be? This is the test. Spiritual healing is the healing of the spirit. It is a new life in the awareness of that which God wants us to be. It is letting God regenerate us into healthy souls. It is living on that high spiritual plane where the physical is relegated to its proper place, where health is natural because the heart is whole, and where God is able to empower us to triumph over all that life may bring. Somewhere in his writings, Brother Mandus has said: "Divine Healing is not only some spasmodic prayer that might make us whole in a second. Divine Healing inevitably is a way of life in which we unfold this glory of the Christ Being within as a daily experience of ever-increasing and joyful adventure in the Kingdom of God."

12.
When You Are Healed

The train from London stopped longer than one might expect at such a little station. An unusual number of people got off and they got off slowly and painfully, for there were many cripples and obviously sick ones among them. Then it was not easy for them to board the bus, but soon we were winding our way along narrow roads banked by hedgerows and overhung by ancient oaks. I could feel the pressure of anticipation building up while we waited in the large, pleasant room of the rambling old manor house. Promptly at the appointed hour, he came in and began his work in silence. One by one, they sat before him to receive his healing touch, administered with unseen direction and unmistakable love. Some were assisted to the chair, but walked back to their seats unassisted, their faces bright with hope and lined with grateful tears. He left as silently as he had entered, and soon the bus was filled again for the long journey home.

Yet something terribly important, I felt, had been left out. This world-renowned healer had missed the opportunity, and even more, the duty, of relating the healing to

God who gave it. No chance was given to express thanksgiving to God. No suggestion was made regarding witnessing to others about what God had done. No opportunity was afforded whereby the healings that came might be put to work in grateful service to others. No word was said about the necessity of a spiritual change accompanying the physical betterment. No warning was spoken about avoiding the physical or mental or spiritual patterns that probably caused the ailment. In fact, I was so disturbed over the important aspects I felt were lacking, that I mentioned them in the private interview that followed. No satisfactory answer was given. It seemed to be sufficient that the people came for healing and that all had received a treatment that either healed them or improved their condition. But I came away asking myself, "Is this spiritual healing?"

Very often people inquire, "What preparation is necessary before coming to a service of spiritual healing?" You should come hopefully and expectantly, with a faith strengthened by earnest prayer and the reading of some of the healing miracles of Jesus. Then you will enter into the atmosphere of divine love fully aware of God's care. The healing power touches your life. You are lifted up in praise and thanksgiving.

Is that all? Is there to be any difference in you as you pass through the door to face a cold, doubt-ridden world? It is inconceivable that a confrontation with the living God should not change one's outlook upon life, nor fail to create a new disposition toward others so noticeable in the practical and common ways of everyday life that our companions at home and at work will wonder — and be glad. As the sincere worshipper leaves the door of the church, all the world should look different because he is different. Count Tolstoi described his conversion as the experience of a man walking along a road, then stopping and turning around and going in the opposite direction with the sights and scenes that had been on his left now on the right and those that had been on his right now on the left. And Masefield added a triumphant note to the change that came to Saul Kane:

> The bolted door had broken in,
> I knew that I had done with sin,
> I knew that Christ had given me birth
> To brother all the souls on earth.
>
> O glory of the lighted mind,
> How dead I'd been, how dumb, how blind.
> The station brook, to my new eyes,
> Was babbling out of Paradise,
>
> O glory of the lighted soul. [1]

How complete the joy if "God's loving action on every part of your nature" brings about as great a change — when you are healed!

Be sure that your healing is of the spirit. Consider the healing that has come, in whatever form and to whatever extent, as a symbol of an inner, spiritual change. This is vitally important because you are primarily a soul and its healing has eternal value.

If we consider the psychosomatic sources of so many of our sicknesses and even accidents, and realize that

---

[1] John Masefield, "The Everlasting Mercy," *Poems* (New York: The Macmillan Co., 1964), p. 118.

these causes reflect a deeper sickness of the soul, then it becomes essential that we both desire and receive the healing of the spirit. Anything less only palliates the real problem and offers false hope. Spiritual surgery may be necessary. Forgiveness for faulty ways of living and thinking and believing must be sought in sincerity. Then, with the help that God alone can give, a new pattern of life will have to be followed with earnest determination, if the emotional attitudes that led to the ailment are to be avoided. How pertinent here is the warning Jesus gave to the man who had been healed at the Pool of Bethesda: "Look, you are well now. Quit your sins, or something worse may happen to you" (John 5:14).

This points to the advantage of the ministry of healing in the church. There one can find the means of continuing grace through the sacraments along with the inspiration and instruction of the regular services of worship. Pastoral counseling will be available for special needs. A prayer group or a Bible Study Class will afford a close fellowship with others who are concerned. The services of spiritual healing will provide additional teaching as well as a continual reminder of the relation of your healing to God. Indeed, the church is an indispensable opportunity when you are healed.

"Remember Lot's wife!" (Luke 17:32). This warning by Jesus refers to the Genesis story (Gen. 19:1-26). Lot, attempting to escape the destruction of the wicked cities of Sodom and Gomorrah, was told not to look back; "but Lot's wife behind him looked back, and she became a pillar of salt" (Gen. 19:26). Whatever connotations may be read into this ancient account, the warning, "do not look back" (Gen. 19:17) has sound meaning today.

Its psychological and spiritual meaning is as needed as it is obvious. There is a bit of the hypochondriac in all of us, and we are familiar with the bore who always wants to tell about his most recent operation. To dwell upon the minute details of a previous sickness hinders the process of healing. Morbid thinking about the past nullifies our power to move forward. When you are healed, "look not behind thee," but look ahead to a life of new and greater dimensions.

Very often a person who has received a special blessing of healing has asked, "Should I tell anyone about it? I remember that Jesus warned those whom He healed not to tell it abroad." This statement is not wholly true, for there are some recorded healing miracles of our Lord in which no such warning occurs. The confusion is confounded by several instances in which such warnings are given, but for no apparent reason, as in the healing of a deaf and dumb man (Mark 7:31-37), of two blind men (Matt. 9:27-31), and of Jairus' daughter (Matt. 9:18-26; cf. Mark 5:21-43; Luke 8:40-56).

On the other hand, it is an interesting study to see what the full story reveals as to the reasons for such warnings in some other accounts. In the healing of a leper, found in all three Synoptic Gospels (Matt. 8: 1-4; Mark 1: 40-45; Luke 5: 12-16), the obvious explanation is that Jesus wanted him to show himself to a priest in the Temple at once in obedience to the ancient Mosaic law. To tell others before receiving the certification that he was no longer a leper not only would endanger him, but would thwart the operation of a good and just custom. The warning to the many who were healed (Matt. 12:15-21) would seem to indicate a necessary limitation of Jesus' ministry to the Jews if He was to fulfill His Messiahship, according to the proof-texts that Matthew adds. While no admonitions are given, some accounts of the miracles clearly indicate that Jesus' healing ministry was a compulsive compassion incurring considerable risk. It encouraged His enemies to seek signs rather than to accept His truth (Matt. 16:1-4). It interfered with His training of the disciples, so that on one occasion, He took them all the way to the coast of Phoenicia, but the healing of the Canaanite woman's daughter (Matt. 15: 21-28) caused Him to be recognized, and the multitudes pressing upon Him made it necessary for Him to return to Galilee. It increased the danger that He might be taken before His work was done (Matt. 12:1-14).

On the positive side, there is more than enough support for answering the above question with a resounding, "Yes. Tell it abroad! Give your witness of what God has done for you. Glorify Him in every way with humility and thanksgiving!" Read again and again the stories about the healing of the paralytic (Matt. 9: 1-8), of blind Bartimaeus (Matt. 20: 29-34), of the deaf and dumb man (Mark 7: 31-37), and about the exultant praise of the multitudes when they were healed (Matt. 15: 29-31). In two instances — that of the blind man of Bethsaida (Mark 8: 22-26), and of the paralytic just referred to — Jesus told them to go home, knowing that they would give their witness there. The sequel to the healing of the demoniac in the country of the Garasenes across the Sea of Galilee includes a definite command (Matt. 8: 28-34; Mark 5: 1-20; Luke 8: 26-35). Naturally, the man wanted to stay with the One who had saved him from his desperate state, but Jesus said, "'Go back home to your family and tell them how much the Lord has done for you, and how kind He has been to you!' So the man left and went all through the Ten Towns telling what Jesus had done for him; and all who heard it were filled with wonder" (Mark 5: 19b-20).

There is an understandable reticence about telling others of a healing that has come to us. Some fear that others will think them a bit too holy or simply queer. There are always those who are too ready to criticize such testimonies as premature or unrealistic. It is natural to succumb to a "wait and see" policy. Good judgment and common sense have a rightful place, but an unreasonable delay may foster doubts. Consider how limited Jesus' ministry would have been if no one of the healed had told about it. Probably the multitudes would not have pressed upon Him as they did, and not nearly as many would have heard the truth He came to preach.

It is imperative for you to give your testimony of what God has done for you, especially in a day when God so often is thought of as being remote and disinterested, or even "dead." The need for help is greater than ever, and the harassed and distressed of humankind crave for the assurance of a God who cares. Hear the bidding of the psalmist:

> Then they cried to the Lord in their trouble, and
> he delivered them from their distress;
> he sent forth his word, and healed them, and
> delivered them from destruction.
> Let them thank the Lord for his steadfast love,
> for his wonderful works to the sons of men!
> And let them offer sacrifices of thanksgiving,
> and tell of his deeds in songs of joy!"

Psalm 107: 19-22

When you "tell of his deeds in songs of joy," you never know how far-reaching your influence will be, or what unrealized good may be accomplished. In thinking about the uncounted number of people healed by Jesus, one is brought to the conclusion that the rapid spread of the gospel and the increase of believers could be accounted for, in large measure, by those who were healed and by those who witnessed the miracles — all acclaiming with joy the One now proclaimed and worshiped as the Christ of God.

One reason for the influence of Christian Science is the Wednesday evening testimony service. It would be a valuable contribution if the services of spiritual healing included opportunity for such witnessing. The doctors should be given credit, too, for the help afforded by their treatments. And of course, the healing should be verified by every means of medical science.

Several times, Mrs. W. had come many miles to attend our Healing Mission held every Sunday afternoon, and was one of our most faithful Prayer Partners. Then suddenly faced with the necessity of an operation for a malignant tumor, she insisted upon being brought to the church to attend the Mission at that time being conducted by Brother Mandus of England. I quote a few sentences from her letter written to me some weeks later:

"It seemed that the Spirit flowed warmly through Brother Mandus into me. . . . I awakened in the recovery room in the usual 'fog,' but had no pain.

"The first night after surgery, I had discomfort, but no pain. . . . I had nurses, nurses' aides, and so forth, coming in to see the post-operative patient who had had no pain-medicine and was going home the third day after surgery. My special nurses said they had never had a patient before who had done this, and to each of them I told about the prayers for me, about the healing service at Emmanuel and Brother Mandus. . . .

"One of my nurses also told me she had been trying hard for years to find God. When she left me the day I came home, she said, 'You have helped me to see more clearly for myself, and I will pass on to my patients what I have seen with my own eyes. I would like to be a Prayer Partner.'" [2]

The words of witness must be followed by deeds of dedication. Often, as I have seen people eagerly coming for the laying-on of hands at healing services, I have been strongly tempted to ask, "Why do you want to be healed? What will you do with the blessing of health if it is bestowed upon you?"

What could be more practical than to begin where you are? This means that you will assume again the responsibilities of life at the point where your daily duties were disrupted by illness. If they had been distasteful, and frustration lay at the seat of the causative tension, now you will discover a new motivation to enlighten the former drudgery. If you tended to enjoy overmuch the care and attention with which you were surrounded during your illness, even this will be counteracted by a resurgent zest for life and the satisfaction that comes from a new sense of self-reliance. A realistic example is found in Jesus' healing of Peter's mother-in-law, "who was sick in bed with a fever . . . and he went to her, took her by the hand, and helped her up. The fever left her and she began to wait on them" (Mark 1: 30-31; cf. Matt. 8: 14-15; Luke 4: 38-39). The common round can be glory-crowned!

---

[2] See Appendix.

Since all healing comes from God, why not dedicate the gift of health to the service of His church? In the "fellowship of the concerned" surely there can be found outlets and opportunities for the trained or undiscovered abilities of those inspired to *noblesse oblige* by a thankful heart. Even a person who still has some disabilities which may handicap his activity can participate in the discipline of praying for others, under the guidance of a prayer group or an alert minister.

Somewhere I heard the story of a woman who received the blessing of new health through the ministry of healing in her church. At once, she became a very devout and active member of the prayer group. When a change in her husband's business made it necessary to move to a distant city, she sought out the nearest church of her denomination, but was keenly disappointed to find that there was no prayer group and no interest whatsoever in the healing ministry. For a time she was tempted to attend another church, but finally decided to make the first church her church home and to try to find some way of serving in the realm where she felt she could make the most vital contribution. It was not long before she realized that the people of the parish were losing interest and some members were leaving because of the poor preaching. The young minister, although well trained and sincere, was sadly ineffective in the pulpit through lack of confidence. The dwindling congregations pulled him down into a slough of complete discouragement. He openly hinted at leaving the ministry. In one of her devotional periods, a plan unfolded to our friend. The very next Sunday, she was at the church thirty minutes before the hour of the service and found a secluded seat behind a pillar. This went on for weeks. One day, her closest friend, whose duties brought her to the church early, wrung from her a confession as to why she came so early and sat alone. "So that's why our minister is preaching better!" the friend exclaimed. "I never thought our prayers could help the preaching. Let me join you. And let's get a few more, too." Thus, the person who had been healed and knew the power of prayer through her own experience sought and found a unique way to put that power to work. It was an opportunity for service as well as an offering of thanksgiving.

Sometimes the opportunity for service is more prosaic. The day before our women at Emmanuel were to conduct their annual bazaar, the stranger who came across the city to attend our services of spiritual healing brought in a shopping bag containing seventeen aprons she had made. The story behind her offering is best told in a letter she wrote to me shortly afterward: "Four weeks ago, I started attending Emmanuel's Spiritual Healing Mission. At that time my hands were swollen, fingers stiff and fast becoming useless. The arthritis had gone into my arms, shoulders and neck. Constant pain and sleepless nights were routine. Because of a serious cardiac condition, the only medication given was aspirin. Since coming to Emmanuel, the pain and stiffness have left and my hands are supple and useful once more. With all the release from pain, tension has lessened and the cardiac condition improved. Since no new medication, therapy or diet had been given, I am sure it was brought about through God's mercy and the prayers at Emmanuel's Healing Mission." Her healed hands, "supple and useful once more," had found a very practical way in which to express her gratitude by making seventeen aprons!

And some are healed to heal. What greater work of

thanksgiving for the blessing of healing than for the healed one to become an instrument for the healing of a rift in a church or organization, or to render a positive influence for bringing about a friendly feeling in a neighborhood or community that has been torn apart by dissension; or to heal the deep wounds of rivalry, jealousy, and misunderstanding among friends, relatives, in a marital break, or in the home! For spiritual healing is infinitely more than the healing of a body. It signifies the presence of a power great enough to heal *all* of our broken relationships. It can be a mighty leaven of love to raise the level of life all about us to a higher plane.

It is not unreasonable nor beyond belief to expect that God's healing power will flow through the healed one to heal others. No greater miracle, I believe, has been recorded in our time than the restoration of life that came suddenly to Dorothy Kerin, who was at the point of death after years of suffering. She was awakened out of sleep by a wonderful light all around her, and a figure spoke out of the light: "Dorothy, you are now quite well. God has brought you back to use you for a great and privileged work. In your prayers and faith, many sick shall you heal; ... "[3] She "was not disobedient to the heavenly vision," and became a modern mystic with healing in her hands. Through guidance in prayer, she established a number of prayer-oriented nursing homes in London before obtaining beautiful "Burrswood" in Kent, with its miracle-wrought Church of Christ the Healer.

When you are healed, whatever you do, be humble!

---

[3] Dorothy Kerin, *The Living Touch* (Taunton, England: Wessex Press, 1948), pp. 17-18.

God takes a tremendous risk in healing the bodies of certain people because they are so liable to lose their souls in spiritual pride. A "holier-than-thou" complex negates the value of the witnessing, and does damage to the Christian concept of God. Christ stooped to touch a leper, and knelt to wash the feet of the disciples. Always remember that spiritual healing is the healing of the spirit, too. It is never earned and never deserved. Like God's grace, the gift is given that you may serve humbly in His Name and for His sake.

And be thankful! There is no true healing without the grace of gratitude. In the story of the healing of the ten lepers (Luke 17: 11-19), only one returned to give thanks and he then received the second blessing of spiritual wholeness. The therapy of thanksgiving is both proof of real healing and the best preventive against the re-currence of the ailment. That wonderful "young" lady of eighty-two, mentioned before (p. 80), once wrote me a choice note beginning with these words: "Years ago, George Herbert wrote:

> Thou that has given so much to me,
> Give me one thing more, a grateful heart.

It is indeed a grateful heart that thanks you for the intercessions you have made for my hands; and a joyous, loving heart that gives thanks to our Christ who has granted the intercessions."

What resounding praise will fill our churches when the people sing their thanksgiving for the ministry of healing! So convinced am I of the therapeutic value of gratitude that I always begin the healing period in every service of spiritual healing[4] with the giving of thanks, asking each one to express inwardly his thanks to God for one special blessing, as we remain in silent prayer; and than I invite all to join in a prayer of thanksgiving usually introduced by the exultant words of the Psalm 103 (vv. 1-5):

> Bless the Lord, O my soul; and all that is within
>   me, bless his holy name!
> Bless the Lord, O my soul; and all that is within me,
>   bless his holy name!
> Bless the Lord, O my soul, and forget not all his
>   benefits,
> Who forgives all your iniquity,
> Who heals all your diseases,
> Who redeems your life from the Pit,
> Who crowns you with steadfast love and mercy,
> Who satisfies you with good as long as you live
> So that your youth is renewed like the eagle's.

To say that our times are out of joint is a truism, but the fact is desperately true. Our ideals are broken into a thousand pieces and our thinking is disordered. Even our ideas of God and the fundamentals of our faith are being assailed on every hand. The very structure of our civilization is fractured by competitive and empowered ideologies. The body of mankind is being dismembered by a recrudescent racism. The sense of utter hopelessness concerning the world situation has infected whole segments of the population with the poison of rebellious self-centeredness. The disorganization of life around us is the

---

[4] See Appendix.

cause of a dangerous disquietude in human personality. Dr. Paul Tournier is so right when he claims that "disease and death are symbols of the disorder that has broken in upon the world as a result of sin."[5]

On the other hand, people make environment, and the conditions of a civilization reflect their inner attitudes. Since these are largely prompted by the emotions, the response of people to life governs the state of life around them. In his chapter on "Psychosomatic Disorders," Dr. White of Harvard University ends with this significant statement: "Neither the disorders of the body nor the disorders of the world can be cured without reference to problems of emotional adjustment."[6]

To be healed is to be called to the cause of world redemption. The economy of God's grace is always purposive. The experience of spiritual healing creates a new faith in God and in life, with its accompaniment of peace and poise and power. Instead of fear and every kind of maladjustment, there grows confidence and conviction. With God, you form a partnership, and your witness carries the weight of His known presence into a world that is like a flock of sheep without a shepherd. Begin where you are, and with what you have. You will find that the opportunity for influence will be matched by the increase of resource. Never consider yourself as unimportant — as a "poor little me." Instead, think what God can do with one perfectly dedicated person.

---

[5] Paul Tournier, *A Doctor's Casebook in the Light of the Bible* (New York: Harper & Row, 1960), p. 205.

[6] Robert W. White, *The Abnormal Personality* (New York: Ronald Press, 1948), p. 451.

God wants you to be well. His desire for you is an abundant, joyful life. His will for you is that you be a radiant witness to His love and care. His purpose for you is that your wholeness contribute to the healing of a sick and broken world.

God's power within us makes possible the Kingdom of God.

Appendix:
The Service of
Spiritual Healing

Since some readers of this book will not have attended a healing service of any kind, while others will be familiar with varied forms of such services, it seems good to append a brief description of the service to which I have frequently referred. For our purpose now, it does not seem necessary to discuss the merits of different forms of services or to offer the reasoning behind this one, so I simply give in outline the order used at our Sunday afternoon services in Emmanuel Episcopal Church, Cleveland, Ohio.

Worship. A hymn. Several brief prayers and the Lord's Prayer. Announcements. Offertory hymn, during which the small cards, given to the people at the door as they come in, are collected. On these cards, they have written the *first names* of the persons they desire to have included in the intercessions.

Instruction. A Scripture lesson, followed by a brief address. Whether long or short, this latter is vitally important. For most people, spiritual healing requires a revolution in their thinking in regard to God as One who cares, to Christ whose ministry of compassion continues, to the Holy Spirit as the beneficent power of God still at work in the world, to the efficacy of prayer, and even to the validity and relevance of the Holy Bible in our day. I believe that an address should be included in every service of spiritual healing, for, without such constant teaching and inspiration, the people will not be able to appreciate fully the value of the healing ministry, nor be led to participate in its benefits.

HEALING PERIOD

Thanksgiving. It may seem strange to begin this climactic period in the service with the giving of thanks, because most of the people in attendance are so full of their troubles that they have little room for gratitude. Introversion and self-centeredness are among the devilish concomitants of sickness. All the more need then for a strong reminder that there is always something for which they can be thankful. God is still good and He still cares! Indeed, there is therapy in gratitude. Praise and thanksgiving represent the highest form of prayer. Therefore, the people are invited to give thanks to God for *one* blessing during a half-minute of silence. This is followed by the reading of Psalm 103:1-5 or some other passage or verse of praise, and then a prayer of thanksgiving.

Intercessions. Prayers for others precede prayers for ourselves. The cards on which the people have written the names of those for whom they desire intercessions have been placed on the altar. In the middle of, or following, an intercessory prayer for the sick, the names are read, with a pause after each one so that the people in the congregation can repeat the name. The purpose of this is to gain the participation of the people, to make each one feel that he is responsibly sharing in the prayer for all the names as well as the ones he wrote on his own card, and to develop through such audible means the total force of prayer-power in the church. The response is always general and wholehearted. The effect is positively awesome. Usually several other prayers follow, but always there is one for doctors and nurses.

The Laying-on of hands. Having voiced our thanksgivings and prayed for others, we are ready to ask God's healing for ourselves. This step is introduced by this prayer:

> "O living Christ, draw nigh to us now, as we draw nigh to Thee, and in this quiet and sacred hour be Thou the hope and peace of our souls; make us conscious of Thy healing nearness. Touch our eyes that we may see Thee; open our ears that we may hear Thy voice; enter our hearts that we may know Thy love. Overshadow our souls and bodies with Thy presence, that we may partake of Thy strength, Thy love, and Thy healing life. Amen."

Then, kneeling at the altar and placing my hands upon it, I whisper this personal prayer of dedication:

> "O Lord, take my mind and think through it. Take my heart and set it on fire with love. Take these hands and through them bring to these, Thy suffering children, the fullness of thy healing power."

Rising, I turn to the people and give the gesture of

invitation with extended open arms. The organ begins to play softly a medley of old, familiar hymns. According to previous instructions, the people who desire the ministration come forward and stand in the aisle no closer than the first pew. One by one they kneel at the far ends of the communion rail. Approaching each one alone there, I ask his first name and "What shall we pray for?" Then, laying hands upon his head — or sometimes upon his eyes or ears — I pray extemporaneously, in a low voice, including in the prayer the request that has been made and using his name perhaps several times. He is dismissed with the words: "Arise and go in peace, and may the peace of God go with you."

Sometimes there is some personal word relative to his specific desire or need. During this time the people in the congregation, according to previous instruction, are praying for each person as he receives the laying-on of hands. Again, this feature seeks to secure the participation of the people. It gives them something creative to do during what otherwise might be a long period of inactivity on their part. It makes each one feel that what is taking place at the communion rail is his responsibility as well as the minister's. It engenders Christian love and sympathy as it dramatizes the Christian community gathered together with its sick in its midst. It adds tremendously to the force of prayer power. And the minister is supremely conscious of a wave of spiritual strength coming from the congregation as he administers this ancient and sacramental rite. When all who desire this ministration have come forward, the organ music ceases and I conclude the service with several brief prayers and the blessing. The people go out in silence.

It is recognized that a service of spiritual healing in connection with, or included in the Holy Communion, would not require the opening worship as given above, but I insist always that a brief address of teaching and inspiration come at the beginning of the actual healing service. Then the three steps of the healing period follow: Thanksgiving, Intercessions, and the Laying-on of hands.

In regard to the felt presence of an almost over-whelming degree of spiritual force or prayer-power brought about by the earnest praying of the people present in the church, another feature must be noted. The inauguration of the Emmanuel Healing Mission, as it was called, every Sunday afternoon at four o'clock seemed a greater task than I could ever handle alone. There was no time to organize and train a prayer group to undergird the effort, and I needed many people to help with their prayers and to sustain the attendants at the services. In a moment of high intuition I conceived the idea of having Prayer Partners. A letter was sent to all on the mailing list of the parish as well as to others who had evinced a particular interest in our healing ministry. This explained the purpose of the Mission and included a return card indicating their willingness to attend every Mission service *or* to spend at least a part of that hour in prayer for the service. The card contained a special prayer which would be a guide for their meditations. The response was overwhelming for such a new venture. Eventually there were nearly five hundred signed Prayer

Partners representing almost every denomination and many states, and also Canada. Of course, not everyone could be expected to attend every Sunday or even to keep the prayer tryst at that hour. However, so many did participate with faithfulness and dedication that the very atmosphere of the church was surcharged by the devotion of those unseen "pray-ers."